"FROM WITHIN"

DEVON WILFORD-SAID
AUTHOR/HUMBLE SERVANT

This book is a work of non-fiction. Names and places have been changed to protect the privacy of all individuals. The events and situations are true.

Copyright © 2021 by Devon Wilford-Said.

No part of this book may be reproduced, stored in a retrieval system, or transmitted by any means, electronic, mechanical, photocopying, recording, or otherwise, without written permission from the author.

ISBN: 978-1-952302-43-5 (sc)
ISBN: 978-1-952302-44-2 (e)

Library of Congress Control Number: 2021902157

TABLE OF CONTENTS

Dedication xi
Acknowledgements and Courtesy Contributions xiii
Preface xv
About the Author xvii

Chapter 1
Quiet Time Meditation (Part 1) 1
Quiet Time Meditations 1
A Move in the Spirit 2
Devon's Expressions 3
Expression of Spirit 4
Intimacy w/God through Praise and Worship 5
One in Spirit 7
Spirit Lifted 8
I Speak unto You 9

Chapter 2
Quiet Time Meditation (Part 2) 11
Wisdom 11
Rejoice 12
Silence 14
Great is the Lord 15
Praises 16
A Mind Stayed on the Lord 17
Precious Jewel 18
Restore Us Again 19

Chapter 3
Quiet Time Meditation (Part 3) 21
Strong Embrace 21
The Word of Life 23

Safe in His Arms 25
Heed the Call 26
Spiritual Journal Series 27
Quotes 29
Blow the Shofar in Zion 31

Chapter 4
Spiritual Wisdom and Insight 33
Freedom from Bondage 33
Who is this…Jesus is Lord? 37
The Way, the Truth and the Life 39
Rejoice and Be Glad 43
Knock and the Door shall be Opened 44
Words of Instruction 46
Thoughts from Within the Mind 48

Chapter 5
Exhortation and Affirmations (Part 1) 51
Reach Out from Within 51
Blow as the Wind 52
Words of Exhortation 53
Sharing 55
A Faithful Exhortation 56
Joy in the Spirit 57
The Planting of the Lord 58
A Message of Love 59
Perpetual Sins 60

Chapter 6
Exhortation and Affirmation (Part 2) 61
Let Go of Stress 61
A Letter to My Heavenly Father 63
Decree of Agreement 65
Established in the Faith 66

The Love of God 67
The Mind of Christ 68

Chapter 7
Spiritual Poems/Prose Song Poems/Lyrics (Part 1) 69
Praise Worthy..69
My Song of the Night..71
Wisdom 72
Glory to the Lord 73
Spirit..75
Words 77

Chapter 8
Spiritual Poems/Prose Song Poems/Lyrics (Part 2) 79
We Shall Walk...79
The Spoken 80
Question: Why We are Here?..81
Testing the Waters 82
Humbly Pray 82
That Place..83
Imagine 84
Be Renewed 85

Chapter 9
Spiritual Poems/Prose Song Poems/Lyrics (Part 3) 87
The Stillness of Silence...87
The Quietness of Silence...87
When Day Turns into Night..88
Abba, Father Hallelujah..89
Vision of Victory...90
A Prayer for Healing 91
The High Place..92
In My Mind's Eye 93
Come Away 94

Chapter 10
Spiritual Poems/Prose Song Poems/Lyrics (Part 4) 95
Life Goes On..95
Praise the Lord 96
Revive 97
Where Angels Fly 98
Evening in Flight...99
Words Embrace 100
Shine Down on Us 101

Chapter 11
Creative Expression (Part 1) 103
I Exist and I Am Word 103
What Do You Fear?...104
Dream My Dream 106
What Happens When?...107
Live Life..108
Spring Forth 109
I Am Grateful.. 110
Rejoice O' Earth.. 111

Chapter 12
Creative Expression (Part 2) 113
What's Happening... 113
Today... 115
My Days.. 116
Quiet of Time 117
Miles Ahead.. 118
Feelings 119
Do You Know?..120
Alive.. 121
Breathe into Spring 122
The Light...123

Chapter 13
Prophetic Utterance 125
Prophetic Utterances 125
Confirmation of the Lord's Divine Presence 125
An Exhortation of Hope 128
Prophecy 129
Last Days Prophecy 130
Hidden But Not Secret 132
Keep the Faith 135

Chapter 14
Thoughts Prayers/More Poetry (Part 1) 137
Knock and the Door shall be Opened 137
The Lord's Peace 139
His Love for Us 140
Trees of Righteousness 141

Chapter 15
Thoughts Prayers/More Poetry (Part 2) 143
Pray without Ceasing 143
Who Am I? 145
From Within 147
Think About It 149
Author's Closing Remarks 151

DEDICATION

"And be renewed in the spirit of your mind."
Ephesians: 4: 23 KJV

    This book is dedicated to the chosen of God and readers who enjoy reading creative expressions of the Spoken Word, biblically inspired writings of prayers, song-poems, and lyrics—and other inspirational literature that allows us to take a journey of exploration from the heart into the very mind of the Spirit that is, *"From Within"*
    It is also my hope that each reader finds peace, joy, and total fulfillment during their quiet moments and that this book continues to be an inspiration for many more years to come.

                      --Min. Devon Wilford-Said
                        Author/Humble Servant

ACKNOWLEDGEMENTS AND COURTESY CONTRIBUTIONS

Special Thanks To:
My Late Beloved Husband
Minister Ahmed B. Said
Prophetic Utterances
"Confirmation of the Lord's Divine Presence"

Sister and Friend in the Faith
The Late Evangelist Lucinda Adhikari
Poem Entitled: "Praises"

PREFACE

Theme: *"A Word Spoken in Season from Within Strengthens the Body, Soul, and Spirit."*

This book was inspired by the Holy Spirit of God to minister to souls needing to be encouraged and set free in the spirit of their minds. It was designed to inspire and transform one's negative ways of thinking into positive thoughts that escape the fear of the unknown.

The spiritual exhortations and affirmations, poems/prose, prayers, lyrics/song-poems, and prophetic utterances will lift up the heads of the downtrodden and bring hope to hopelessness and despair.

This book will harness the depth of one's spirituality and totality for understanding life.

Most readers will be suddenly touched by the beautiful words of inspiration and creative expression and tap into their own spirituality. #

ABOUT THE AUTHOR

Ms. Devon Wilford-Said, Minister, Prophetic Teacher/Scribe, Author/Poet, is a native of Martin County, North Carolina; and presently resides in Baltimore, Maryland. She is a widow indeed and has one daughter and two beloved grandsons.

Devon graduated from Writer's Digest Schools Inc. Class'1985 Cincinnati, Ohio. She attended Dominion Bible College formerly the Mid-Atlantic Bible College Logos Urban Bible Training Institute where she received most of her biblical education studies and training during her tenure as an active member of First Apostolic Faith Church of Jesus Christ, International located in Baltimore, MD.

Ms. Wilford-Said is spirit-filled and called into the body of Christ according to her faith occupies various gifts and talents in the areas of teaching and instruction, lay-exhortation, intercessory prayer, the prophetic realm and serves as an armor bearer to support others. She is presently affiliated with the First Philadelphia Baptist Church of Baltimore, MD. And, presently teaches women and men of the faith and new disciples in The Gathering: Small Group Bible Study Fellowship for Women and Men of the *"The Church without Walls"* Prophetic End-time Ministry located in Baltimore, MD.

Devon enjoys writing inspirational literature such as poetry and prose, memoirs, short stories, and aspires to prosper in the field of writing. ###

CHAPTER 1
QUIET TIME MEDITATION (PART 1)

"QUIET TIME MEDITATIONS"

Relax, release, and relate to the stillness that surrounds you and from within you.

Read a book, take a walk, sit still for a few minutes, and enjoy the silence.

Embrace the joy of laughter, and express your creative juices.

Take a long hot bubble bath, close your eyes, and feel.

Take a journey in your mind to a beautiful faraway place.

Praise the creator of all things and rejoice.

Listen to the stillness of water that flows from a mountain stream.

Sing a melody from your heart and allow love to radiate from it.

Reach out on a beautiful spring or summer day, and smell the roses.

Remind yourself that love surrounds you and that you are loved.

Enjoy your 'Quiet Time Meditation' and take more time.

Whenever needed to sustain and renew your inner spirit for each day.

But most of all allow peace to reign from the depths of your soul always and share

Peace Be unto You!

"A MOVE IN THE SPIRIT"

There's a move in the spiritual realm that has released an atmosphere for divine healing, and miracles; prosperity, and success for those of you who believe in the impossible ever being made possible by your faith in the Highest God; there's an opportunity for increase so stop, right now—close your eyes, breathe in and inhale the Lord's sweet grace, love, and mercy! Trust Him to work out all of those ruff places and dark areas of your life.

Release all pain and sadness, hurt feelings, grief and sorrow, and your confused way of thinking; receive your breakthrough from the realm of Spirit and of Life.

Rejoice in your time of renewal and refreshing; thank God for giving you His wings of victory that enables you to fly over those troubled waters of strife—And now your mind is clear with peaceful thoughts as you relax, release, and relate to the newness of life. Go ahead and celebrate your freedom. Walk in the Spirit, rejoice, and remain faithful! #

"DEVON'S EXPRESSIONS"

"Today I Rise"

Today, I rise and kiss the dawning of a brand-new day…Today, I rise and hope for all things good and lovely to come my way! Today, I rise to embrace the unknown with true faith and love…Today; I rise to give all thanks to my Maker from the heavens above!

"Embraced into His Light"

The intense stare of his gaze left my heart pounding with expectancy as his eyes pierced straight through my soul; and the voice of his words echoed life abundant to me as the roaring sound of rushing water hitting against rocks from a mountainous river stream. His unconditional love was expressed with such quietness for that one moment in time; and then he reached out for me and embraced me into His light. Selah.

"I Will Speak Good"

I will speak of good times and of pleasant things…I will say to the hearers that which edifies and that which encourages. O' mouth speaks words of wisdom, knowledge, and that of understanding to listening ears that it may be said, "The words that I speak are Spirit and life."

"Breathe In"

I close my eyes and breathe in pneuma, "the breath of life" and sigh with relief to let go of toxic waste from all sinful impurities, and I breathe in life and exhale death and know that the purified agape love from Yeshua's blood washes me clean from within and without! Selah.

"EXPRESSION OF SPIRIT"

Deep within the inner depths of the soul, I evoke His Spirit
Thoughts of divine emotion entangled
against the backdrop of imagination
As manifold blessings are manifested from the Spoken Word—
I've lifted from temporal situations and
marked toward heaven's plane
Agape love and totality from life now embraces my being,
As tears stream down—from a joyous face
peering above the darkness towards light
Deep within the inner depths of the soul, I evoke His Spirit
Thoughts of love, peace, and goodwill
fights against negativity's control
Angelic beings all around while hearkening
to the voice of His Words—
I've elevated now from earth's atmosphere
towards the ethereal heavenly realm
High praises and satisfaction from within now absorb my soul,
As tears continuously stream down—from a joyous
face reaching out to embrace Spirit #

"INTIMACY W/GOD THROUGH PRAISE AND WORSHIP"

The Spirit of the Lord is ushering his people into His presence…We must open our hearts and release our spirits to connect with His. Below is an illustration of a closer and intimate relationship with our Almighty "Abba" Father. This can be done during your quiet time or at any time you feel led to so. I pray that you are blessed by the outcome.

* Begin by lifting up your hands in an outstretched motion with the palms facing forward.

* Bow your head ever so slightly…and say this quick prayer of affirmation.

Heavenly Father in the name of Jesus, I thank you for the opportunity to present myself to you. Please forgive me for any transgressions that I have committed knowingly or unknowingly at this very moment. I repent and ask for your forgiveness right now, and believe by faith that I'm forgiven.

Lord God, I want the more of you…my soul thirst for you. Fill my cup to the overflow and allow me to get to know you better. You are my life…my strength and salvation. I love you, Lord! You are the lifter up of my head; and I exalt you with the highest praise of Glory Hallelujah! Release me and set me free to praise and worship you the more. In Jesus' name, I pray, amen.

* Now close your eyes and think about his goodness. Begin to speak to him and tell him who he is to you. Thank him and praise him for who is…

* Sing spiritual psalms unto him…speak words of praise from the scripture, or from scripture memory.

* Clap your hands and thank him…offer up to him a heave offering which is swaying your arms from side to side before his presence. Rejoice and allow the Holy Spirit to lead you more into His presence.

* Remember to chant the glory hallelujah praise over and over…He loves this it's like a sweet swelling savor of frankincense and myrrh. The smell of your praise identifies your submission to the throne room. So, go up…go up higher and release your worries and stresses of this life. Allow the Spirit to take you up higher! The Lord is saying to you now, come up here and I will show you great and wonderful things that you know not! Think of the thing that is of a good report; think about these lovely things…love, peace, kindness, faith, joy, meekness, longsuffering, etc.

* Now that you're within the secret place of the Most High…allow Him to minister back unto you…and be still and know that He is God! Amen…

"ONE IN SPIRIT"

Love conquers hate
Spirit gives life
Peace instead of war
Mind is over matter
Faith brings prosperity and success
Life unfolds its beauty
Spirit reveals truth
Giving supersedes receiving
If gravity's weight is lifted
Spirit begins to soar
Agreement brings unity
Power of thought
Sets forth change
Compassion overcomes sorrow
Joy brings gladness
A "good tree" bears "good fruit"
You are what you believe
And Spirit cannot be bound…#

"SPIRIT LIFTED"

Let your spirit be lifted
Reach high from down below
Let your spirit be lifted
Do not hinder where it goes
Let your spirit be lifted
To find out what it sees
Let your spirit be lifted
It's destined to be free…#

"I SPEAK UNTO YOU"

I speak unto you love, good health, success, peace, and joy—
That you with each passing day may embrace life the more
I speak unto you God's favor, spiritual gifts,
And talents to be used that you with
His strength will be healed and never abused;
I speak unto you prosperity, good dreams,
Hopes fulfilled and brand new
That you may walk in faith and believe
That's nothing is impossible unto you
I speak unto you abundance that you can achieve—
That you may know that all things are yours
If you would only dare to believe!"

CHAPTER 2
QUIET TIME MEDITATION (PART 2)

"WISDOM"

The ancients once spoke from times passed as a voice of one crying in the wilderness; What shall I do, and what can I give in hopes of determining the right choices for living? With an ability to know by seeking knowledge—what shall I do once it has been found?

How do I comprehend what I have learned and distinguish right from wrong, and truth from error? Do I accept or disregard the information that was received? There's so much to know but without an understanding; knowledge alone can be so fruitless. "Wisdom is the principal thing, but with all our getting we must understand."

"REJOICE"

Rejoice O' daughters and sons of nations, for you shall inherit the good of the land. After we have conquered the demands of our flesh, our spirit shall creatively soar and rise above our circumstances.

Pondered thoughts are creative images from the mind's eye and spirit, waiting to be manifested into the natural realm of space and time. Overcoming denotes a conquering spirit as does faith the hope for salvation. #

"From Within"

"ATTITUDE"

I can be happy, mellow, or sad—
May be green with envy and sometimes mad
I can be up, down, or even in between
I can tease, be loving, and also very mean
Or like a computer that's gone out of whack!
I can give a smile, and or take it back
Attitude…

I can yield to the left, or stay on the right
I can be cool as a cucumber, or even uptight
I can be nice, considerate, and easier to get along
Or scream and shout, if you dare get me wrong
Attitude…

I can be as an ocean tide, high or very low
Negative or positive, or however you know
I can be witty, loving, and even enthused
Sometimes bored, less exciting and crying the blues
Attitude

Only you can determine just how I shall be
For I live your emotions where the heartstring pulls me
If you keep me up, and on a positive spree
Then I'll be well behaved, less moody and free;
Attitude…

This Poem is dedicated to (Mrs. Betty Vaughn A Dear Friend)

"SILENCE"

Loud voices echoed noises surrounded me
amidst the backdrop of time;
Whisperings that could not be uttered and
babblings left misunderstood
I heard words that were inaudible, and in
a language spoken by the angels
What shall I do? How should I respond, and what would be said?
If I dare spoke the words aloud deep withinside me;
Then another voice sounded with a hush that whispered softly
Silences…silence…silence! #

During Quiet Time Meditation
DWS—July 2004

"GREAT IS THE LORD"

Great is the LORD, and greatly to be praised!
Amid creation, kindred tongues of every nation;
From the valley below to the mountain's top
Let the high praises resound and never stop
Great is the LORD! Great is the LORD!
Hallelujah! Great is the LORD!
Shalom.
--Devon Wilford-Said

"PRAISES"

In my praises I'm in the presence of the
LORD the one whom I adore;

In my praises, there's love, peace, strength, and
joy—for every woman, man, girl, and boy

In my praise's strongholds come down and
there's another star added to my crown

In my praises, I give God the highest praise, Hallelujah! Hallelujah!

So, when you're going through, I recommend this to you—

Give God some praise; Hallelujah! Hallelujah! #

Inspired by: "The Holy One"
Written by: "The Gifted One"
--Evangelist Lucinda Adhikari

"A MIND STAYED ON THE LORD"

Keep your minds stayed on Him;
When trouble has oppressed with hopelessness
Keep your minds stayed on Him;
When fear and doubts set in and sadness begins

Keep your minds stayed on Him;
Despite the pain of starting over again
Keep your minds stayed on Him;
Don't give in to displeasures or loss

Keep your minds stayed on Him;
Persevere and be steadfast with faith at any cost
Keep your minds stayed on Him;
And trust in the Father from on High!

"PRECIOUS JEWEL"

Shimmering gold dust which sparkles in place

Surrounds the circumference of her beautiful face

In-depth knowledge from visions of old

Stories from times past that must be told

"From Within"

A Poem of Tribute
In Memory of Dr. Martin Luther King, Jr.

"RESTORE US AGAIN"

Restore us again, and soothe us with your love;
Restore us again and heal aching wounds from times past
Restore us again massage our hurts and the pain
Restore us again with your oil of gladness
Restore us again with family and friends
Restore us again and teach us to sound wisdom
Restore us again with love abundant; forevermore
Restore us again in a better place for healing
Restore us again—Restore us again

CHAPTER 3
QUIET TIME MEDITATION (PART 3)

"STRONG EMBRACE"

Our Beloved reached out his hands from
above and touched the essence of all
By night his eyes shine as bright as the stars—
pierced deep amidst the darkness
By day his glow radiates as the golden sun
with warmth for all who's near
With arms outstretched, he welcomes
everyone within his strong embrace
He gathers the masses to an ark of safety
against life's toils and anguished fair
To a faraway place that's hidden from sight-
--and alas without a care
Our Beloved reached out his hands from
above and touched our very soul
By the light of his face and burnished brass
skin---that glitters fine and sure
By way of amber flames of light, he pours
out his love for all that fears—
With arms outstretched, he again welcomes
us within his strong embrace
He gathers the masses into an ark of safety
against life's evils and demands
To a faraway place that's hidden from sight—
and alas the righteous stands
Our Beloved reached out his hands from
above and touched the essence of all

Devon Wilford-Said

By night his eyes lead as bright as the stars-
--pierced deep amidst the darkness
By day his glow radiates as flames from candle
wax melted down onto the floor
With arms outstretched, he again welcomes
us within his strong embrace
He gathers the masses to an ark against
life's storms and times of despair
To a faraway place that's hidden from sight-
--and alas without a care
Within his strong embrace…#

"From Within"

"THE WORD OF LIFE"

Abba Father, your Word sustains life and brings vitality
I trust your Word to give us victory throughout all eternity
Your Word is light and it directs our path into righteousness

Abba Father, I thank you for your Word
because it teaches us all truth
I thank you for your Word because it's our weapon of warfare
Used to pull down strongholds and bring every disobedient thought
To the obedience of Christ when our obedience is fulfilled

Abba Father, your Word brings forth
healing of body soul, and spirit
I thank you for your Word because it
satisfies our need for completion
I thank you for your Word because it offers hope
To and for unbelievers when they accept the LORD by faith

Abba Father, your Word harnesses
goodness, strength, and fortitude
I thank you for your Word because without it we cannot stand
I thank you for your Word because its truth brings freedom
From all bondage's, especially the bondage of sin

Abba Father, your Word helps me, and many others
To commune with you and worship you in Spirit and in Truth
I thank you for your Word because we also delight ourselves in you
I thank you for your Word that holds the earth on its axis
I thank you for your Word because after everything else fails
Your Word shall be left standing forever

Abba Father, I thank you for your Word and pray
That we continue to meditate daily in it and hold fast to it to
I thank you for your Word, and shall for the rest of my life and days
Keep holding forth the Word of Life from you!

In Jesus Name,
So be it and Amen.

"From Within"

*In Loving Memory of
Her Beloved Father Mr. Earl Wilford*
Dedicated to His Daughter:
Mrs. Deanna Wilford-McDaniel

"SAFE IN HIS ARMS"

The Lord looked down upon her solemn face
As she slumbered, and slept quietly in her bed;

He then sent an angel to embrace her and covered her
With protection throughout the darkness of night;

When she'd arise up the next day during early morn and at sunrise;
She felt his abundant love and joy, which had been left as a gift

How amazed was she at His presence knowing
That it was He as she slept through the night

Her mind had savored the warmth of His touch and His embrace
It was as if she'd been showered with pure
love and the abundance of peace.

I say unto you, "rest, rule and abide with Him as He is with you,
And live on in His Peace.

*"And the peace of God which surpasses all, understanding
Shall keep your hearts and minds through Christ Jesus our Lord!"*
Philippians: 4:7 KJV

Amen…

"HEED THE CALL"

"Come up here my beloved; and refresh
your souls from the issues of life.
Come up here my beloved; and keep your
tongues from misery and strife.
Come up here my beloved; and turn away from all sin.
Come up here my beloved; if you open
your hearts then I'll come in."
"Yeshua, Ha'Machiach—Jesus the Christ the
Anointed One of Yahweh, GOD"
--March 2011

"From Within"

SPIRITUAL JOURNAL SERIES

Foundation Scriptures:

"Hearken (listen) unto me, O house of Jacob, and all the ***remnant*** of the house of Israel, which are borne by me from the belly, which are carried from the womb: And even to your old age I am he, and even to hoar (gray) hairs will I carry, and deliver you." **Isaiah: 46: 3-4 KJV**

GOD'S REMNANT: (THE CALLED CHOSEN AND THE FAITHFUL)

"THE THREE WAVES OF THE SPIRIT"

Wave No 1: Preparation and Focus: (Equipping the Called, Chosen, and Faithful)
"And saying, Repent ye: for the kingdom of heaven is at hand. For this is he that was spoken of by the prophet Esaias, saying, the voice of one crying in the wilderness, ***prepare ye the way of the Lord***, make his paths straight." Matthew: 3: 2-3 KJV

"If my people, which are *called* by my name, shall humble themselves, and pray seek my face, and turn from their wicked ways; then will I hear from heaven, and will forgive their sin, and will heal their land." II Chronicles: 7:14 KJV

Wave No. 2: The Manifestation of God's Glory to the True Worshippers
"And the glory of the Lord shall be revealed, and all flesh shall see it together: for the mouth of the LORD has spoken it." Isaiah: 40: 5 KJV

"And the Word was made flesh, and dwelt among us, (and we beheld his glory, the glory as of the only begotten of the Father.) Full of grace and truth." John: 1: 14 KJV

"For the earnest expectation of the creature waits for the ***manifestation of the sons*** of GOD."
Romans: 8: 19 KJV

"But the manifestation of the Spirit is given to every man to profit withal." I Corinthians: 12: 7

Wave No. 3: Prepare for the Coming of the LORD (End Time Release)
"Therefore, thus will I do unto you, O Israel: and because I will do this unto you, ***prepare to meet your GOD***, O Israel." Amos: 4: 12 KJV

"Behold, the LORD GOD will come with strong hand, and his arm shall rule for him, and his work before him. He shall feed his flock like a shepherd: he shall gather the lambs with his arm, and shall gently lead those that are with young." Isaiah: 40: 10-11 KJV

"Verily I say to you, there be some standing here, which shall not taste of death, till they see the Son of man coming in his kingdom." Matthew: 16: 28 KJV

"QUOTES"
BY
DEVON WILFORD-SAID

"My eyes are opened to see in the Spirit; my ears are attentive to the Voice of his Words as He speaks; my arms are opened to embrace His unconditional love, and my mouth shall sing aloud His praises forevermore."

April' 2010

"I went up high to a faraway place in my mind and could not comprehend the entire beautiful splendor my eyes beheld right before me. I had risen far above the beggarly elements of this world and soared like an eagle from above! For behold, I was now free."

May'2010

"My people come to you, as they usually do, and sit before you to listen to your words, but they do not put them into practice. With their mouths they express devotion, but their hearts are greedy for unjust gain. Indeed, to them, you are nothing more than one who sings love songs with a beautiful voice and plays an instrument well, for they hear your words but do not put them into practice. "When all this comes true—and it surely will—then they will know that a prophet has been among them."
(Ezek 33:31-33 NIV)

"In the spirit of the day thoughts race with bubbling enthusiasm and faith to perfect that which is expected...which is always the unexpected."

Jan'2011

"My eyes looked to the hills and my help came suddenly in a moment and in a twinkling of an eye. I was ever so humbled when He lifted me up high in the Spirit far above principalities and powers and circumstances. That I began to shout the victory that is always in Christ Jesus my Lord! Yes, I will sing praises unto Him and bless His Holy Name forever, Hallelujah!"
Selah.

Feb'2011

"From Within"

"BLOW THE SHOFAR IN ZION"

Behold He shall come with trumpet sounds, and the clouds shall unfold at His entrance!

Yes, the LORD our King—He is the King of kings and LORD of lords;

He shall come quickly. Lookup for your redemption draws nigh!

He is the Word of God and Prince of Peace;

The Sword of the Spirit shall cut down all enemies against the knowledge of the truth

Every knee shall bow, and every tongue shall confess that Jesus Christ is LORD!

Amen and Amen.

CHAPTER 4

SPIRITUAL WISDOM AND INSIGHT

"FREEDOM FROM BONDAGE"

Peace and Blessings Readers:
The purpose of this message is for the lost and I pray that the eyes of their understanding be opened that they may come to the revelation of the truth of who can set them free from the bondage of sin.

"The *Spirit of the Sovereign Lord* is on me because the LORD has anointed me to preach good news to the poor. He has sent me to bind up the brokenhearted, to *proclaim freedom* for the captives and *release from darkness* for the *prisoners,"*
—Isaiah: 61:1 NIV

Would You Like to Know the Answers to the Questions Below?

1. Are you a prisoner of crime and violence, lust and desire, selfishness and greed, hatred and malice, substance abuse and addictions—or are you bound by delusions of grandeur, mind-bending confusion, faultfinding, and racial prejudice?

2. Do you feel trapped inside a body that's contrary to which you are?

3. Do you judge others unrighteous fret often about nothing, gossip, and slander others, and feel lost and alone?

4. Do you believe that God does not exist because you're closed-minded to the truth that He does?

5. Do you wonder why no one seems to like you at times, or are you afraid, and feeling hopelessly lost?

6. Are you at the point of no return, drunkard, and or grief-stricken?

7. Are you resentful and bitter from deep hurt and or sexual abuse?

8. Do you constantly feel that no one loves you and that you're better off dead?

9. Are you haunted by family line curses that need to be broken?

10. Do you harbor unforgiveness and pride?

11. Do you feel that there's no way out of your circumstances?

"FREEDOM FROM BONDAGE"

If you've answered, "yes" to any of these questions then it's your time for salvation! You need to know that the Lord Jesus Christ came to set you free from everything, he gave his life that you may have life; and that more abundantly.

You don't have to suffer any longer from the bondage of sin because Jesus has paid it all.
So, what you need do to be rescued from the demons that often plague your mind with evil thoughts would be to accept God's unconditional love for you, and call on the LORD.

The Lord says, "For everyone that calls on the name of the LORD, shall be saved."
Romans: 10: 13 NIV

I challenge you to call on him right now. That's your first step to obtaining your freedom.

Now, "the *Word* is near you; even in your mouth and in your heart." You must *confess* with *your mouth* the *Lord Jesus,* and *believe in your heart* that God has raised Him from the dead, and you will *be saved."*
Romans: 10:8-9 NIV

And this is your second step to freedom. You must *repent or turn away from sin and be baptized in Jesus' name, and last but not least be filled* with the *power* of the *Holy Spirit of God* to keep you free! Seek the LORD for a good Bible-based church so that you can continue to *learn and grow in His grace* by faith.

"Peter replied, *Repent, and be baptized,* every one of you in the name of Jesus Christ for the forgiveness of your sins. And you will receive the gift of the *Holy Spirit.*

The promise is for you and your children and for all who are far off---for all whom the LORD our God will call.
Acts: 2:38 NIV

Remember This:
"For God so loved the world that he gave his one and only Son, that whoever believes in him shall not perish but have eternal life. For God did not send His Son in the world to condemn the world, but to save the world through him."
John: 3: 16 NIV

In closing, if you have followed these instructions accordingly then congratulations because *you have now been set free; and the angels in heaven are rejoicing over your salvation and also the Saints of the highest*. May the Father and "Yeshua," Our Lord Jesus Christ bless and keep you always!

"WHO IS THIS...JESUS IS LORD?"

Who is this man that says, "My kingdom is not of this world...?" John: 18: 36 NIV

He is the *"Anointed One"* of God and, Jesus is LORD!

Who is this man that says, "I came into the world, to testify to the truth? Everyone on the side of truth listens to me." John: 18:37 NIV

He is the *"Anointed One"* of God and, Jesus is LORD!

Who is this man that says, "I am the bread he that comes to me will never go hungry, and he who believes in me will never be thirsty..." John: 6: 35 NIV

He is the *"Anointed One"* of God and, Jesus is LORD!

Who is this man that says, "The Spirit of the Lord is upon me because he has anointed me to preach good news to the poor? He has sent me to proclaim freedom for the prisoners and recovery of sight for the blind, to release the oppressed, to proclaim the year of the LORD's favor." Luke: 4: 18-19 NIV

He is the *"Anointed One"* of God and, Jesus is LORD!

Who is this man that says, "Come to me, all you who are weary and burdened, and I will give you rest? Take my yoke upon you and learn from me, for I am gentle and humble in heart, and you will find rest for your souls. For my yoke is easy and my burden is light." Matthew: 11:28 NIV

He is the *"Anointed One"* of God and, Jesus is LORD!

Who is this man that says, "I am the Alpha and the Omega...who is, and who was, and who is to come, the Almighty!" Rev: 1:8 NIV

He is the *"Anointed One"* of God and, Jesus is LORD!

Who is this man that says, "He who has an ear, let him hear what the Spirit says to the churches?" Rev: 3:6 NIV

Jesus is LORD! Amen and Amen.

"THE WAY, THE TRUTH AND THE LIFE"

A True Testimonial of Min. Devon Wilford-Said

In the Holy Bible, Jesus says, *"I am the way, the truth and the life"* ... But I've struggled for many years just to fully understand the reality of that truth. From early childhood to my adulthood, I'd always considered myself to be a *"Seeker of Truth."*

But had many questions about just how to get to God...In fact, I'd read the Bible and wondered why the name of Jesus was mentioned so often. "Jesus the Son of God," and "Jesus the Son of Man; why was Jesus so controversial to mankind? What was the comparison of him, to that of God? There were so many things that I didn't understand about Jesus. But I've always believed in God and would say my prayers at night believing that he loved, and watched over me.

I'd recite, "Now I lay me down to sleep, I pray the Lord my soul to keep if I should die before I awake..." on my knees each night along with the 23rd Psalms. No matter what time I'd gone to bed—that prayer had to be recited before I could settle down, and finally, drift off to sleep. And whenever I had a bad day—I'd look up towards heaven and asked an invisible God—to whom I thought would be always watching over me, and that would assist me with my problems in life. Somehow those things made me feel reassured. After all, to me, God was my Heavenly Father—and only father in the absence of my real biological father.

My mind, through the years of growing up, was constantly invaded with puzzling thoughts and unanswered questions. I've always known that I was linked to God in some way or the other, but I would not traditionally set myself up in one particular religion or form of worship.

My experiences varied with religious customs and belief systems. As a matter of fact, I believe that was the reason…I was drawn to that Pentecostal storefront church back when I was a child. Yeah, I would clap my hands to the music and laugh at the people when they shouted because I had not fully understood why, or even what was going on? After all, to me and my younger sister, they looked awfully funny! But those feelings of curiosity and warmth continued to haunt me and lodged deep within my heart. There was an unquenchable desire to be able to understand my true destiny.

I'd studied many types of religions and various forms of worship— and to my chagrin, some good and plenty were bad especially when left untapped by the true and living God. From studying under Jehovah's Witnesses, attending Baptist churches, and Sunday School to Philosophy Studies of the Essenes, Mayan religion, Taoism, Pragmatic Mysticism, and a host of others. Nothing seemed to quench the yearning in my soul for the real truth. I thought that the knowledge I had obtained were only delusions, designed to throw me off from what was hidden deep inside. Just waiting to be opened, and released through my repentance and acceptance of the Lord.

Back when I was a teen, I had called on the Lord and accepted the confession part of it. But when it came down to going under the water that's when I drew the line mostly because fear had set in.

Many questions had bombarded my mind back then. Such as, why was I able to see in the spirit world at such a young age? And what made me flee from my first 'out of body experience' on that cool autumn's night at the age of seven.

I had found myself hovering over my lifeless body at one moment and then shivering from the cool of the night at the next. And, why had I remembered the experience of being borne? I felt for such a long time, that I had been the only one experiencing those strange things that were happening in my life? I even remembered every spiritual encounter from the darkness and also the light?

Many years came and went and I was left wondering, God, what's happening to me? What was the truth about my unforeseen circumstances? Sure, I'd learned many things, and was pressed to know even more. But what was the logical explanation about those dreams and visions, and my ability to foretell things before they happened?

Why had it been so important for me to say my prayers at night? Also, where had the Jesus equation fit in all of it? I had always addressed God, as Father, or Lord. But I never quite understood the name of Jesus. Yet, I had begun to feel that he must be recognized, and somehow be acquainted with God. Or, it wouldn't have pierced my heart with so much conviction.

When I studied the Bible under the Jehovah's Witnesses, I loved the Word of God, But I never fully understood what, *"Paradise Lost, and Paradise Regained,"* meant? Or why they had not recognized the man, *"Jesus"* as the mediator for God? Their principles had been so confusing, and conflicting. So much so that I'd finally grown into maturity and asked God for myself to show me the real truth; and grant me wisdom, knowledge, and understanding. I needed to know him and to my chagrin, he answered my prayers.

I had finally decided to rededicate my life and confessed my sins unto God. But, the courage to be baptized in the name of Jesus came later around June 24th, 1985. Back in the fall of October 1986; I was filled with the Holy Spirit of God, and spoke with other tongues as the Spirit gave utterance. It was a fluent unknown language and dialect from heaven and I had felt so much better than ever before!

My body had spiritually lifted off the floor of the altar that Sunday afternoon and an electric blue mist surrounded me as tears streamed down from my face. I felt as light as a feather on the way back to my seat when the glory cloud of the Lord had momentarily filled the entire sanctuary. My belief in the awesomeness of GOD—and of the power in the name of Jesus whose name meant, "Salvation to God," had finally awakened my mind to the real truth.

Christ, which means, *"Messiah"* or the *"Anointed One,"* was the Heavenly Father's mediator sent to deliver man from his sins and relay His message of love to all humanity. Yes, I understood now that I was one of God's chosen vessels that He gave His Holy Spirit to dwell inside. But, most of all I knew that no man could get to the Father except he is first drawn and led by the spirit through his *Anointed*, Jesus or Yeshua in Hebrew.

Not only had I understood the importance of how to relate to Jesus as Lord because of his status with God. But I knew that we as a people must acknowledge him in everything that's about life and godliness. The Holy Spirit was sent as the comforter from Jesus, and now teaches us and bears witness with our spirit that we are the Sons and Daughters of the Highest, and that we belong to Him.

Yes, the real truth about Jesus had now set in and I was no longer fooled by the many voices spoken in the world. I had now identified with the real true voice that had always been within my heart and his name is—JESUS who is, *"The Way, the Truth, and the Life."* #

NOTE: This testimonial came from the mind and heart of the author based on her personal life experiences, and struggles to find the hidden truth of her spirituality.

"REJOICE AND BE GLAD"

My friends, delight yourselves in the LORD, and He shall grant you the desires of your heart! Bow down before His presence and worship Him! Yes, the LORD is good, and His mercy endures forever!

Call out to Him while He is near! And He will answer you! Let the wicked forsake his way, and turn to his way everlasting! Pray without ceasing, and yield your members to obey His will. Clap your hands, *"rejoice and be glad"* and shout out with joy forevermore!

"KNOCK AND THE DOOR SHALL BE OPENED"

"Ask, and it will be given to you; seek and you will find; *"knock and the door will be opened to you."* For everyone who asks receives, he who seeks finds; *and to him who knocks, the door will be opened."* Matthews: 7:7-8 NIV

"Here I am! *I stand at the door and knock.* If anyone hears my voice and opens the door, I will come in and eat with him, and he with me." Rev: 3:20 NIV

When I first began to seriously get into the Word of God, I found that one of my favorite scriptures was at that time found in the Book of Matthew, Chapter 7; and verses 7-8.

Yes, it was all about the "asking, seeking, and knocking" which led me to believe that God was truly listening to my many prayer petitions to him as a child. Back then my mom had told me and my sisters to read the 23rd Psalm and to recite our nightly prayers for protection. You know that familiar prayer that most children had to say before going to sleep each night.

> *"Now I lay me down to sleep, I pray the LORD, my soul to keep;*
> *And if I should die before I awake; I pray the*
> *LORD, my soul to take."* Amen…

My grandmother once said that I was a special child; and that I was called out for the LORD's purpose. She constantly told me not to fear, but to always trust in the LORD. When I first opened the door of my heart to allow the LORD to come in, I was around twelve years of age.

It was a wonderful feeling of love and acceptance and making that choice was the best thing I could ever do. When I was baptized and filled with the Holy Spirit some years later, I was overjoyed and very thankful that I had done the right thing and made the right choice.

I hope that anyone who may be reading this message, and who has not yet answered the LORD's call that they'd reconsider; and open the door of their hearts and allow Him to come in.

"WORDS OF INSTRUCTION"

Fight the Good Fight
I say unto you my Sisters and Brothers in the LORD, "Fight the good fight of faith and lay hold to eternal life, whereunto you are also called, and has professed a good profession before many witnesses."
I Timothy: 6:12 KJV

A Good Confession
"I give you charge in the sight of God, who quickens [makes alive] all things, and before Christ Jesus, who before Pontius Pilate witnessed a good confession."
I Timothy: 6:13 KJV

Keep the Commandment
"…Keep the commandment without spot un-rebuke able, until the appearing of our Lord Jesus Christ. Which in time he shall show, who is the blessed and only Potentate, the King of kings, and LORD of lords. Who only has immortality, dwelling in the light which no man can approach unto; whom no man has seen, nor can see: to whom be honor and power everlasting." **Amen.**
I Timothy: 6:14-16 KJV

Warn the Rich to Do Good"
Charge them that are rich in this world, that they are rich in good works, ready to distribute, willing to communicate: Laying up in store for them a good foundation against the time to come, that they may lay hold of eternal life."
I Timothy: 6:17-18 KJV

Stir Up Your Gift without Fear
"Wherefore I put thee in remembrance that you stir up the gift of God, which is in you, by the putting on my hands. For God has not given us the *"spirit of fear"* but power, and love, and of a sound mind."
II Timothy: 1:6-7 KJV

The Servant of the LORD
"And the servant of the LORD must not strive, but be gentle unto all men, apt to teach, patient; in meekness [humility] instructing those that oppose themselves if God peradventure will give them repentance to the acknowledging of the truth. And that they may recover themselves out of the snare of the devil, which are taken captive by him at his will."
II Timothy: 2:24-26 KJV

Be Strong and Endure Hardness as Good Soldiers
"Thou, therefore, my son, be strong in the grace that is in Christ Jesus. And the things that you have heard of me among many witnesses, the same commit you to faithful men, who shall be able to teach others also.

Thou, therefore, endure hardness, as a good soldier of Jesus Christ. No man that war entangles himself with the affairs of this life; that he may please him who has chosen him to be a soldier. And if a man also strives for masteries, yet he is not crowned, except he strives lawfully. The husbandman that labors must be partaker of the fruits. Consider what I say, and the LORD gives you understanding in all things."
II Timothy: 2: 1-7 KJV

Be you examples of the grace and mercy of the LORD our GOD in Christ Jesus. Prove all things, and hold fast to that which is good. Pray without ceasing, and always be opened to hear what the Spirit is saying to the Church, and quick to obey into righteousness.

Remember, as you walk…to walk in and by faith; and when talking let your conversation be chaste and seasoned with salt that it may be well-pleasing to the hearers.

"THOUGHTS FROM WITHIN THE MIND"

Life is indeed short and sometimes trying to get by presents many challenges to even just exist. We are in constant motion to find out something about it—the what, when, where, and how questions seem to bombard our intellects. Then there's time there's never enough time to do and complete the intricate details of trying to figure out what to do next. So, we find ourselves in a hurry, always in a hurry to get it done the what, when, where, and how chases us with more and more unanswered questions until many of us find ourselves doing things we never would do.

Oh, it's adolescent, and oh we can't believe it but adulthood has arrived; and there's still not enough time to get it right. And the mind and our thoughts just keep on racing until we've grown up and now have finished high school, gone to college, made new friends, planned a new career, gone out on dates, and found a new mate; started a family, bought a new house, and well trade in the old car for a new one all the while helping to raise the children.

Inhale and exhale and take another deep breath, keep out the nosy neighbors, deal with the household bills—and stop the shopping, shopping, and more shopping! Run up the credit cards and gets into more debt.

Curse out the politicians that you put into office for not looking out for your interest—then breathe in again…hold it and let out! Secure your family from crime and violence out on the streets—keep up with current events and oops forgot to take out the garbage.

Purchased a new computer because the old one has crashed out! Update and upgrade never forget to upgrade. Gone on vacation and remembered the porch lights were never turned on and what about the security alarm system? After all, we must keep out the bad guys and set the alarm for the intruders!

Have we taken some time to smell the roses? It's beautiful earth yes, despite the mass pollution from car exhausts, factory and mining waste, hazardous plastic materials, and those awful emissions from nuclear waste; and what about the Creator have we taken enough time out for Him, and loved our neighbors and do ourselves? Or is beauty only skin deep?

Oh, but there is beauty in all life forms and something special and unique about all things.

We only need to understand that the only true way of living an honest and wholesome life is showing unconditional love—and sharing our blessings with others in need.

Have we taken care of our bodies and prepared for that day of eternal rest? Oh, no…We're distracted, from distractions and more distractions! Thoughts are flying high now and heart races and skips a few beats. No, that can't be the end of it of all. Must take out some more time now to do the right thing. But thought keeps racing; blood flow is pumping and beads of perspiration are rolling down the face—wait, wait a minute grabbing the head! Got to shut off the *thoughts from within the mind* to ease the burdens of stress and time…It can't be too late inhale sob and cry and with hands lifted call on the Name of JESUS just before you die!

Selah. #

CHAPTER 5
EXHORTATION AND
AFFIRMATIONS (PART 1)

"REACH OUT FROM WITHIN"

There's a way that we all can change the world *from within,* and that is by exploring our true nature from inside—

I believe that inside every one of us lies something so unique and beautiful that it often yearns to be able to, *"reach out from within,"* and to enhance our lives in this present-day world;

Despite what we may be feeling about ourselves at times—we still can reach down from the core of our being and spark that wonderful light of love placed there to explore the many wonders for change;

It starts from the common ground of our understanding of just who we are, and why we must co-exist here together in peace and harmony to avoid self-destruction;

When we come to terms with this reality and our purpose for living; then we can begin to explore new possibilities for making a difference in our world starting with ourselves…#

--July 20, 2004

"BLOW AS THE WIND"

"To truly know what's in the world of spirituality
One must become spirit—and just blow like the wind"
Swoosh…swoosh…swoosh…
Always keep a smile, and you will be happy"

DWS-- July 22, 2004-2020

"WORDS OF EXHORTATION"

Rejoice and be glad in the LORD for this is the season for rejoicing! Though the storm clouds keep raging and the enemy tries his best to hinder. We have the victory to overcome all these things. The Lord is with us, and is in us!

The LORD of Hosts, the Mighty God, the Prince of Peace, the Alpha & Omega and Beginning and Ending, Jehovah Jireh our Provider shall be with us and provide for us always; so again, I say, Rejoice, for the LORD our God is Mighty and He shall save us!

We are His people and the sheep of His pasture; He will keep back no good thing from them that love Him and walk uprightly. The LORD our GOD is our battle-ax, He will war on our behalf, and when the enemy comes after us one way, they shall flee from us seven ways.

The LORD's eyes watch for us and go to and fro the earth on our behalf; He sees all and knows all; there's nothing hidden from Him in whom we have to do. Rejoice and be glad for the LORD our GOD is strong and mighty in battle!

The weapons of our warfare are not carnal, but mighty through Him to the pulling down of all strongholds. We are more than conquerors because He loves us. So, walk upright, repent daily, and confess your faults one to another that you may be healed.

Pray one for another because of the effectual and fervent prayer of the righteous avails much! Believe and stand on the Word of God and have faith in GOD! Jesus says that He'll never leave us nor forsake us! Believe the Father's WORD always.

Walk by faith and continue to live by faith! We shall obtain and we shall apprehend the hidden mysteries since the world began. For the Father has promised to reveal them to us. Wait patiently on the LORD and He shall give you the desires of your heart.

Remember to always praise and worship Him in Spirit and in Truth and rejoice, again, I say rejoice! Selah.

"SHARING"

We communicate our ideas, our dreams, our hopes, our intentions
and our desires;

We embrace our true feelings from being able to speak
that which is lodged deeply inside;

And once our words have entered into the earth's atmosphere
We anticipate the response which oftentimes follows;

From our sharing— #

"A FAITHFUL EXHORTATION"

I believe that the sole purpose of mankind is to glorify the Creator and to enjoy Him forever. The Lord God wants a personal relationship with his people even though some may not believe that he truly exists.

To accomplish such a task, one must have faith. The ability to believe in something or someone that cannot be seen; and an act of believing the impossible. We can't see the wind, but we believe that it is there when we see trees move, and sway back and forth when it blows. We can feel the wind on our faces but yet it is still invisible to the naked eye.

The Lord our God is Spirit, and cannot be seen by the human eyes; however, His presence can be made known just as the wind does after it blows. Or through and by us when we began to express our love and compassion for each other. We cannot see love physically but we can feel it as we embrace one another both naturally and spiritually.

"Now faith is the substance of things hoped for, and the evidence of things not seen." Hebrews: 11: 1 KJV.

Faith, *"Now faith"* the faith that's right now. The will of God is for us to have at least a measure of it to believe. "The substance of things hoped for… that hope is the *fervent expectation* that faith has created something out of nothing by our belief in the impossible.

God has made it possible to prove our purpose for living in the first place.

…" *For we walk by faith, and not by sight."* God is…who he says He is, and He is *a rewarder of them who diligently seek him.*" We must walk in faith and by faith, believing.

If our purpose for living is to glorify God, then we must have the faith of God to maintain that purpose for living. I encourage everyone to pray for that kind of faith and watch for the miraculous to happen in your lives when you dare to believe. (Shalom)

"JOY IN THE SPIRIT"

During these last days of everything under the sun that's happening to us; and sometimes against us time after time. I say to you, there's hope and I embrace you all with the Spirit of Joy!

I know you may say how can I speak about joy when there are so many uncertainties and unanswered questions about our lives? Sure, we wake up some mornings feeling good about ourselves; and the next day or even during that same day our world will start to cave in on us.

Oftentimes, there's misplaced confidence and reassurance due to societal changes, family issues, and quality time spent with the Creator for spiritual renewal and cleansing. Our hearts may be heavy from dealing with the pressures of life such as preparing for the holidays, taking care of our children, maintaining a safe and secured environment in a dangerous society, or trying to fight against a life-threatening illness, and or diseases.

Yes, we have many negatives that surround our lives and that may increase doubt for the future. But I say unto you that the agape love which comes from the Almighty covers each and every one of us. And all we need do is to accept it, and embrace the *"Joy in the Spirit"* that was provided for us to keep us strong!

The "Joy of the LORD," is our strength! I say unto you all be joyful even despite what you may be going through. There are hope and peace that comes from within and His agape love is the key to keep us going! Be blessed...#

"THE PLANTING OF THE LORD"

Have you ever planted a seed and watched it grow into something beautiful? I mean by actually, nurturing it… watering it, feeding it with plant food and at times having to prune away it's dead and discarded leaves of decay? It feels good to be a caretaker of something so fragile and that needs your loving hands to comfort, nurture, and protects it from life's storms etcetera, doesn't it?

Well in comparison that's how many of us are spiritually born, raised, and nurtured from and by the LORD today. We are his *"seeds of righteousness"* once we've come to know and have the right relationship with His Son Jesus Christ, *"The Word of God!"* We are just as connected to the LORD as vines are attached to branches of a tree. We abide in Him, and he abides in us because He is the *Seed of the Word, which* was planted into us from the beginning.

The Word was planted as a seed in our hearts…and was designed to be nurtured, and grown by our faith in God. And through our acknowledgment of and belief in His only Begotten Son, Jesus Christ who came into the world in flesh, suffered bled, and died on the cross, and who rose victoriously on the third day to save us from sin.

Yes, because of what Jesus had faithfully done on the cross he gave us an assurance that we could accept his gift of eternal life to grow up…and become sons and daughters of the Highest and, *"The Planting of the LORD!* #

"A MESSAGE OF LOVE"

I greet you all in the precious name of our Lord Jesus Christ. May his love embrace, comfort, and strengthen your bodies, souls, and spirits during this season of preparedness for his coming. The Lord has inspired me to write this message to inform you of the urgency of his coming.

We must do his "work while it is day because at night no man works." I charge you, "to be strong in the LORD and the power of his might" during the hour of temptation in the earth that sets to try us and our faith. Remember, the LORD is our portion and that he is with us to carry out the responsibilities outlined in our ministries.

We have been pre-ordained for such a time as this to carry out his will in the earth. Our very presence shakes the foundation of darkness. We can destroy the enemy's camp by the WORD of GOD and the power of the HOLY SPIRIT. "For it's not by power, nor by might but by His Spirit, says the LORD of Host."

We must continue to fight the good fight of faith and stand with our full armor of God during the battle. For we know that the battle is not ours but it's the LORD's!

Let us "stand fast in the liberty whereby Christ has set us free, and be no longer entangled with the yoke of bondage," because we are more than "conquerors in the LORD GOD Almighty, and "We can do all things through Christ who strengthens us."

In your quiet time begin to praise and worship GOD. Invoke his presence and bask in His Glory. Sing spiritual songs, hymns, and even a new song with authority, and Praise the LORD with all your hearts. Always remember that "He inhabits the praises of his people."

Stay blessed and free in your Spirit!

Amen and Amen.

"PERPETUAL SINS"

QUESTION: How does one begin to overcome bad habits that they know should be canceled?
And because of the harm, it can do both naturally and spiritually?

ANSWER: In life, we shall have tribulations, and be tempted by the devil however, we must overcome evil with good and abide in the Word of God over the area of weaknesses in our flesh that urges us to continue in our repetitive bad habits.
"The spirit is willing, but the flesh is weak...."

QUESTION: How do we overcome when others continually throw stumbling blocks in our path because of petty jealousies and strife?

ANSWER: The Lord God shines his light down on the just and the unjust, the good and the evil. Overcome evil with good, and do not allow others to steal your joy. Rebuke with all longsuffering, and separate yourselves from workers of iniquity. Pray for those who wrongfully persecute you.

QUESTION: What do we do when we find ourselves falling back into the same path of destruction even after our breakthroughs?

ANSWER: For the believer, deliverance is in Zion; and in your house. If we shall confess our sins, he is faithful and just to forgive us of our sins, and to cleanse us from all righteousness."

"All have sinned and fallen short of the glory of God..."

CHAPTER 6
EXHORTATION AND AFFIRMATION (PART 2)

"LET GO OF STRESS"

Relax, release, and relate to the stillness that surrounds you and from within you;

Read a book, take a walk, sit still for a few minutes, and enjoy the silence

Embrace the joy of laughter, and express your creative juices.

Take a long hot bubble bath, close your eyes, and just feel the calmness overtaking you;

Take a journey through your mind to a beautiful faraway place—and breathe in.

Praise the Creator of all things, and rejoice;

Listen to the stillness of water that flows from a mountain stream.

Sing a melody from your heart and allow love to radiate from it;

Reach out on a beautiful Spring or Summer day, and smell the roses.

Remind yourself that love surrounds you and that you are loved.

Enjoy your *Quiet Time Meditation* and take more time whenever needed to sustain and renew your inner spirit for each day;

But most of all allow peace to reign from the depths of your soul always, and share it!

"Peace Be with You"

"A LETTER TO MY HEAVENLY FATHER"

Thursday, March 9TH 2006
FROM: Devon You Humble Servant/Daughter
TO: Abba, Father My Provider, and Deliverer

Dear, Father:

Today I sat and wondered in which direction I should be going. There are so many opportunities physically and naturally out there for me but my heart and mind is fixed on the spiritual at this particular point in my life.

What would you have me do concerning the mundane issues of this life? Somehow, I am feeling that I'm missing the point. My interest in matters of finding my financial niche in society seems to be staggering and boredom is setting in from the many distractions that come my way from other people's dreams and desires that many times include me and my husband's resources to enable them to obtain it.

Lord, I just want to be able to be at peace with what I do to bring you glory! Give me instruction and or direction for the road that I should take; guide my feet, strengthen my body and renew my mind to stand fast.

Father, without your assurance and favor I can do nothing. My life is like an empty shell.

I enjoy writing, organizing, and ministering to others by example to become closer to you.

Teach me to become more knowledgeable and grant me more wisdom and insight to share me gifts with others.

I love you Lord, and I want to be able to please you with good work while I am able to move, and have my being here on this earth.

I thank you for this moment of quietness and your listening ear to what my heart cries out from within. You are my joy and satisfaction. You are my hope beyond hope.

You are my healer and deliverer. You are my Lord and King! You are my strength and peace. You are my way-maker and rock. I give you the glory that's due unto your name, and I thank you for the opportunity to communicate via this letter to you today.

Father, before I close will you please show me again; and reassure me of your greatness and presence with me? Sometimes I need to be embraced with your protective arms around me.

I need to see your glory and be reassured that I am not alone because I am never alone with you.

Thank you, Lord, I appreciate your love and protection, and until next time when we converse Peace and Glory Hallelujah to you as always, in Jesus' name. Amen.

Shalom,
Your Beloved Daughter
Devon Wilford-Said

NOTE: My letter to the Father was penned during a dry wilderness period in my life when I was being pulled from all directions, going through trials and tribulations, and being unfairly treated by people of the world, and ministers in the faith.

"DECREE OF AGREEMENT"

1. I, (We) decree a closer and more intimate fellowship with the Lord as of today.

2. I, (We) decree reassurance and claim it in Jesus' name.

3. I, (We) believe and receive a more excellent relationship with the Father which is in heaven.

4. The Lord Jesus shall walk with me, and talk with me daily. I, (We) shall hear His voice and know him when He speaks.

5. I, (We) agree to respond to His leadership and counsel only; and be submissive to His will and commandments by faith. He shall give me, (us) in Jesus, name.

6. I, (We) believe and receive by faith all that the Lord shall give me, (us) and give according to that faith we have in it.

7. I, (We) decree a closer walk with God the Father and our Lord Jesus Christ. In sweet holy communion both in this world and in the world to come. I, (We) claim it by faith in Jesus' name.

"Now faith is the substance of things hoped for, the evidence of things not seen." Hebrews: 11: 1 KJV

"ESTABLISHED IN THE FAITH"

"As you have therefore received Christ Jesus the Lord,
So, walk you in Him. Rooted and built up in
Him, and established in the faith,
As you have been taught abounding therein with thanksgiving."
Colossians: 2: 6-7 KJV

INSTRUCTIONS: *Insert the word "I" for*
an Individual and, "We" for Groups

AFFIRMATION

I am rooted in the faith;
I am built up and established as I have been taught
By Jesus Christ (Yeshua' Ha-Messiah) who is my Lord
I abound therein with thanksgiving
I shall continue in the faith
Forever grounded and settled
I will not be moved away from the hope of the gospel
Whereof I, Devon Wilford-Said am made a Minister
(Insert Your Name)

"THE LOVE OF GOD"

"Beloved, let us love one another: for love is of God;
And everyone that loves is born of God,
And knows God
He that loves not knows not God:
For God is Love
In this was manifested the love of God toward us,
Because that God sent his only begotten Son
Into the world, that we might live through him
Beloved, if God so loved us;
We ought also to love one another
No man has seen God at anytime
If we love one another,
God dwells in us, and His love is perfected in us

I John: 4: 7-12 KJV

INSTRUCTIONS: *Insert the word "I" for an Individual and, "We" for Groups*

AFFIRMATION

I am love and made perfect in love;
I love God because He first loved me
And sent His Son for the propitiation of my sins
I love my neighbor as myself
I believe that Jesus (Yeshua) is the Son of God
I do not fear it because I have the perfect love of God
And perfect love cast out fear
My love is made perfect in Him, and I dwell in His love forever; #

"THE MIND OF CHRIST"

"Let this mind be in you, which was also in Christ Jesus"

Philippians: 2: 5 KJV

INSTRUCTIONS: *Insert the word "I" for an Individual and, "We" for Groups*

AFFIRMATION

Let this mind be in you, which was also in Christ Jesus
I have the mind of the anointed of God,
And everything that I believe by faith to happen
It shall come to pass;
Let this mind be in you, which was also in Christ Jesus
My mind is opened to the realm of the Spirit
Because I am Spirit—
Therefore, I am in oneness with all! #

CHAPTER 7
SPIRITUAL POEMS/PROSE SONG POEMS/LYRICS (PART 1)

"PRAISE WORTHY"

VERSE 1   O' taste and see that the Lord is good and He's worthy—worthy to be praised
O' taste and see that the Lord is good and He's worthy—worthy to be praised

CHORUS: Hal—le---lu—jah Hal—le---lu—jah
Hal—le---lu—jah
Our God is worthy—worthy to be praised

VERSE 2   O' taste and see that the Lord is good and He's worthy—worthy to be praised
O' taste and see that the Lord is good and He's worthy—worthy to be praised

CHORUS: Hal—le---lu—jah Hal—le---lu—jah
Hal—le---lu—jah
Our God is worthy—worthy to be praised

BRIDGE
(3 Part Harmonies)
Altos/Bass Singers   O' taste and see—that the Lord is good— (3x- times)
Hal—le---lu—Jah Hal—le---lu—Jah
Hal—le---lu—Jah
And he is worthy—worthy to be praised

Devon Wilford-Said

(Sopranos) O' taste and see—that the Lord is good— (3x- times)
Hal—le---lu—jah Hal—le---lu—jah
Hal—le---lu—jah
And he is worthy—worthy to be praised

(All Voices) O' taste and see that the Lord is good and He's worthy—worthy to be praised
O' taste and see that the Lord is good and He's worthy—worthy to be praised

CHORUS: Hal—le---lu—jah Hal—le---lu—jah
Hal—le---lu—jah
Our God is worthy—worthy to be praised

(Lots of improvisation ending the song) #

"MY SONG OF THE NIGHT"

In the stillness of the early morn; I await his guidance and purpose for my life My heart pants for a word of deliverance from troubles that surround me, and which has begun to plague my soul;

Father, I can feel your presence in, *"My Song of the Night!"* Your sweet dew of inspiration and comfort strengthen me to endure despite what I may be feeling at this the moment; I praise you Lord, and I worship you always—My heart is opened to receive all that you have prepared for my life to be victorious;

I wait on you Lord because in myself I can do nothing; I hope in you O, My God, because there is no better hope: I cry unto you O' Lord because no one else can heal my pain; You know everything there is to know about me and how to fix the broken pieces of my life; And you know how to mend my troubled soul;

For in you, Lord God is my salvation, my joy: In you, Lord God is my peace, and strength; You are the longing in my soul, and a thirst that cannot be quenched by water alone; But you Lord God have restored my soul; When doubt seems to take me over—I find your strength holds me fast into truth and righteousness:

When the issues of life surmount daily with one crisis after another; your Spirit embraces me and comforts me during my weakest moments; For it's you O' Lord my God that confirms the word of your servants: The words that you have spoken are sure and must come to pass!

I thank you, O' my Lord for being my all and all, and for reminding me of who I am in you: For you have given me a conquering spirit to fight and to stand; You have girded my loins with truth and your mercy prevails even when I have fallen short; I thank you for being with me always even until the end of the age: But most of all during *My Song of the Night*, Amen. #

"WISDOM"

The ancients once spoke from times passed

As a voice of one crying in the wilderness;

What shall I do, and what can I give?

In hopes of determining the right choices for living

With an ability to know by seeking knowledge

What must I do once it is found?

How do I comprehend what I have learned?

How do I distinguish between rights from wrong?

And also discern truth from error?

Do I accept or disregard all the information?

That I have received?

There's so much to know;

But without an understanding knowledge

Alone can be so fruitless:

And then I heard whispered in a still small voice

"Wisdom is the principal thing, but in all

Your getting don't forget to get

A good understanding..." #

"From Within"

"GLORY TO THE LORD"

(Slow or Moderate)

CHORUS Glory to the highest—to the Lord Most High
Glory to the highest—to the Lord Most High
Glory to the highest—to the Lord Most High
Glory to the highest—to the Lord Most High

VERSE 1 He is Jehovah Rapha—The Lord that healeth—you
(Repeat 2 times)
He is Jehovah Elyon—He is the Lord Most High
(Repeat 2 times)

CHORUS Glory to the highest—to the Lord Most High
Glory to the highest—to the Lord Most High
Glory to the highest—to the Lord Most High
Glory to the highest—to the Lord Most High

VERSE 2 He is Jehovah Shalom—He is the Lord our Peace
(Repeat 2 times)
He is Jehovah Jireh—He is the Lord that provides
(Repeat 2 times)

CHORUS Glory to the highest—to the Lord Most High
Glory to the highest—to the Lord Most High
Glory to the highest—to the Lord Most High
Glory to the highest—to the Lord Most High

BRIDGE Hosanna Hallelujah—to the Lord Most High
Hosanna Hallelujah—to the Lord Most High
Hosanna Hallelujah—to the Lord Most High

IMPROV Shout Glory—Glory Hallelujah to the Lord Most High
Lead Singer- Shout Glory—Glory Hallelujah to the Lord Most High

Choir	Everybody sing unto the Lord—He is the Lord Most High
	Glory to the Highest—to the Lord Most High
	We sing praises to you Jesus—You are the Lord Most High
	Glory Hallelujah to the Lord Most High
	Glory to the Lord Most High—to the Lord Most High
	(Lots of improvisation ending song)

Revised Lyrics: January'2006
DWS

"SPIRIT"

SPIRIT	Pneuma the breath of life breathed into man by the power and will of the Almighty Creator which made him a living soul;
SPIRIT	The existence of wind an invisible, mysterious, and powerful force that one cannot see, but yet feel as it blows from each direction from the four corners of the earth
SPIRIT	Divine supernatural power, energy, and or the "Ruach" Spirit of life and source of vitality; The Almighty invisible force of the wind which can be transformed for good or evil.
SPIRIT	The divine inspirer of prophets, in essence, the "Spirit of Prophecy" the Holy gift from Almighty God that was given to speak words of exhortation and comfort to His people by way of an anointed vessel in the form of a man or a woman:
SPIRIT	Our key to transporting our minds, and bodies to destinations in a *moment*, and without the use of transport vehicles such as cars, boats, trains, planes, trucks, etc.
SPIRIT	And the Spirit of the Lord says, "Come up hither (here) and I will show thee (you) great and mighty things thou (you) knoweth (know) not."

SPIRIT   Come away with me, and journey into a place into the third heaven; a place no man has seen with the human eye. Fly away…far above the earth's atmosphere and explore the wondrous realm of space and time into eternity.

SPIRIT   The secret shall be revealed through praise and worship and adoration unto the Lord, our Creator as we seek Him with all our hearts.

SPIRIT   Let us go and be at one with Him to a place where mortality is changed immortality, and life has no end even after death!

SPIRIT   ***

"WORDS"

WORDS   The ability to speak and or expose one's thoughts either spoken or written.
I find them to be most intriguing, and powerful, thus reflecting the essence of our Creator. They are to me the desires of one's heart etched into the divine scheme of things, and the creative manifestation of thought;

WORDS   Are intellect, spirit, emotions, and the essence of life. We were spoken into existence by the Word of God; therefore our *"Words"* can be creative.

WORDS   Can build up, tear down, and destroy. They can inspire, enlighten, and mesmerize us with sensual desires of self-expression, and tickle our funny bone with laughter and joy. They can be fundamental, superficial, action-packed, and or psycho-analytic filled with intellect and without spirit.

WORDS   Can be expressed with authority and power when spoken into the atmosphere. They can lift us on a pedestal or tear us down to our lowest low as it relates to self-esteem.

WORDS   They can deliver and set free the captive soul from all types of addictions, and or bondages. They can cast spells both good and evil, cast out demons, or hinder one being delivered from evil influences.

WORDS   Can be positive or negative, depending on how one chooses to use them. So, I would recommend that they be used wisely.

WORDS   Have been given to me as a gift to be expressed by way of exhortation, and encouragement, inspiration, praise, and worship, and by the agape love of God, to speak into the hearts of each reader that perchance may be reading these, *"WORDS."*

WORDS   ***

Revised: April 2011-2020
DWS

CHAPTER 8
SPIRITUAL POEMS/PROSE SONG POEMS/LYRICS (PART 2)

"WE SHALL WALK"

Let us walk down the streets of eternity
Let us walk hand in hand
Let us walk together in unity and oneness
Let us walk in with fortitude and strength
Let us walk with hearts opened to share
Let us walk, as "We shall Walk"

Let us walk high in the air of purity
Let us walk as the time demands
Let us walk together in peace and closeness
Let us walk with spirits lifted free
Let us walk uprightly and let us stand
Let us Walk, as We Shall Walk"
Let us walk with faith that's everlasting
Let us walk as steadfast as we can
Let us walk together in God's love always
Let us walk with high praises and joy
Let us walk forever onward and sure
Let us walk, as "We shall Walk"

"THE SPOKEN"

We speak, and we say whatever that may come to mind;
We speak, with sounds of expression that ignites into time
We speak, and we tell of things from past and present;
We speak, within the core to our very essence
We speak, and time may sometime stand peacefully still;

We speak, in hopes that we are perfecting our Father's will;
We speak, with challenges to each other and often we debate
We speak, sadly with tears and our hearts sorely aches;
We speak, when we have something to say and even if we don't;
We speak, and alas' we shall speak, The Spoken…#

Originally Created: June 2004
Revised: April' 2011

QUESTION: "WHY WE ARE HERE?"

In my Opinion

ANSWER: WE ARE HERE TO:

We're here to glorify Almighty God, and to enjoy Him forever.

We're here to give love and to be loved.

We're here to be fruitful and to multiply, and take dominion over the earth.

We're here to learn and to grow spiritually, intellectually, emotionally, and physically.

We're here to use our minds to explore all possibilities in this life with freedom of choice.

We're here to bond with each other as one in humanity without racial or religious prejudices.

We're here to create and to use our abilities to cultivate the earth for a more healthy living environment.

We're here to give and minister to the needs of one another both naturally and spiritually

as the Father has prospered us to freely give out of our substance...

We're here to make a difference in the world; and also, the universe by way of spreading the message of hope and agape love to all! #

IN LOVING MEMORY OF
Mr. Henry L. Wilford
A.K.A.
(Jake, Sir Henry, and Unc)

"TESTING THE WATERS"

I stepped into the waters of the rivers of life—

To revive my soul from misery and strife

No more pain and suffering to detest

I have now entered into my Father's rest! #

"HUMBLY PRAY"

There are moments in this life that may be wasted away

If we do not take enough time to humbly pray;

Our meditative thoughts and verbal requests

Reflects our ability to give to God our best

Although some answers may be somewhat delayed

We must not give up hope after we've humbly prayed;

Peace

"THAT PLACE"

In the distance and far beyond the horizon;
A light shine so brilliantly as the stars
My heart pounds ever so fast to reach it
That place somewhere above called, home;

In the distance and far beyond the horizon
A ray of hope shines so brightly as the sun
My arms extend ever so far to reach it
That place somewhere above called, home;

In the distance and far beyond the horizon
A city waits magnificently in the sky
My eyes search ever so fast to reach it
That place somewhere above called, home; #

"IMAGINE"

My thoughts are scattered now as I sat here
And ponder about the wonderful things
That one could ever imagine being real;
Life is full of possibilities, discoveries, and adventures
I breathe in to inhale the sweet fragrances of fulfillment
And, joy, I exhale the remnants of uncertainties and
Inner fears of what was once before;
But now old things have passed away and;
Behold, all things have become new.
Because I dare to dream again with a mind
That often wants to just, "imagine." #

"BE RENEWED"

There's a refreshing that's coming from the LORD a sweet quickening of body, soul, and spirit.

There is a joyous celebration to be proclaimed, and your understanding shall be enlightened.

Embrace His goodness, and inhale the sweet-smelling savor of His love. Mount up your wings as the eagle and soar above your circumstance and situations. Reach up and grab the hidden treasures from above and taste in His goodness.

Be Renewed...

There's a refreshing that's coming from the LORD a better way of thinking, and holding fast to His truth. There's an anointing that's being poured out; and the cup of all your needs shall be supplied. Lift your hands and open up your mouths to praise Him. Yes, sing praises to the LORD a better way of sharing and giving that which only you can give.

Be Renewed...

There's a refreshing that's coming from the LORD a day of remembrance and celebration of his love awaits everyone. Reach up and take hold with faith; and He shall increase you even the more with His grace. A better way of fulfilling your destiny has arisen, and favor following your every step. There's a guiding light of His Spirit to light your path and to keep your foot from falling

Be Renewed...#

CHAPTER 9
SPIRITUAL POEMS/PROSE SONG POEMS/LYRICS (PART 3)

Dedicated to the Families/Victims of:
Violent Thunder Storms, Hurricanes, Tornados,
Tsunami's and Earthquakes
In the United States and around the World

"THE STILLNESS OF SILENCE"

Let quietness take hold so still and soft
As we hold fast our sweet surrender
Let humility take over in place of pride
And look to the hills where our help comes

Let us not give up hope because there is always hope
Amid the storms; and the *stillness of silence*
Let us pray, *"Be still and know that He is God"*

"THE QUIETNESS OF SILENCE"

In the quietness of silence
We hear nothingness
And in the quietness of silence
Nothing needs to be said
In the silence of quietness
Hearts open to truth
In the quietness of silence
We shall now be healed… #
Revised: April 2011-2020 DWS

"WHEN DAY TURNS INTO NIGHT"

The day-spring begins and the sunrise brings joy;

Then the sun goes down below the horizon's floor

Evening creeps—a moonlit sky into the twilight

And the mystery of darkness is now within sight;

Let us look to the heavens again in delight

To embrace the evening, *when day turns into night*

Revised: (4-2011) – (11-2020) DWS

"From Within"

"ABBA, FATHER HALLELUJAH"

(Moderately Fast)

[Talk Audibly] "And after these things I heard a great voice of much people in heaven, saying, Alleluia, Salvation, and glory, and honor, and power unto the Lord, our God." **(Revelation: 19: 1 KJV)**

1st STANZA   Lord, Yeshua Ha-Messiah—Yeshua Ha-Messiah—Yeshua Ha-Messiah—We, (I) sing glory to your Name

2nd STANZA   You are our Mighty Father—You are our Mighty Father—You are our Mighty Father—We, (I) glorify Your Name

CHORUS: Hey Abba, Hallelujah—Hey Abba, Hallelujah
Hey Abba, Hallelujah—We, (I) glorify your Name

3rd STANZA   Lord, Jesus you are Messiah—Lord, Jesus you are Messiah—Lord, Jesus you are Messiah—And We, (I) glorify Your Name

CHORUS: Hey Abba, Hallelujah—Hey Abba, Hallelujah
Hey Abba, Hallelujah—We, (I) glorify your Name

BRIDGE
IMPROV   Doo—Doodle—Doodle—Doo—Doo—Doo-Doodle—Doodle—

Clap/ Stomp   Doo—Doo— Doo—Doodle—Doodle—Doo—Doo
to the beat.   We, (I) sing glory to Your Name

CHORUS: Hey Abba, Hallelujah—Hey Abba, Hallelujah
Hey Abba, Hallelujah—We, (I) glorify your Name

(End song with improvisation singing)

"VISION OF VICTORY"

I close my eyes to see visions of things to come
Where wars have ceased and peace increased;
And now we can live on our earth complete

I close my eyes to see visions of things to come
Of daylight bright and the shining of light;
For we now march to the beat of victory's drum

I close my eyes to see visions of things to come
Where the fear has ceased and true love increased
For we stand in victory from the battle we've won…#

"A PRAYER FOR HEALING"

INSTRUCTIONS: Insert the word "I" for an Individual and, "We" for Groups

Heavenly Father:

In the secret place of the MOST HIGH, our healing is free
So, we speak to sickness and disease this blessed decree;

I, (We) stand firm in the faith and boldly renounce evil for good
And speak life over death as the true believers in God should

I, (We) say to the afflicted who has mustard seed faith in the gate
That you shall be made whole as you believe before it is too late

For it is in the name of Jesus that healing power will flow
So, sickness and disease are now cast out—and out it MUST go!

Now, I, (We) say to you in Jesus Name, that you be made whole;
Thank the Lord; and tell someone just open your mouth and be bold!
Give the glory to our Heavenly Father and let your testimony be told!

I, (We) thank you, Lord, in Jesus Name I, (We) pray.

Amen.

"THE HIGH PLACE"

The journey was not far and I had now reached my destination;

What will He say unto me; as I stood there before Him?

The awe of His Majesty glistened with radiant light;

I was now caught up in that light, and it warmed my very soul

Time had stood still for what seemed like an eternity;

Before I had realized that time, it was not;

For in His High Place—time does not exist;

But we just live in the moment…only at the moment! #

"From Within"

"IN MY MIND'S EYE"

In my mind's eye—I see visions of light that pierces the darkness of the soul

In my mind's eye—life is sure as the moonlit sky

In my mind's eye—No longer am I limited by earth's gravitational pull

In my mind's eye—I can fly endlessly through time and beyond

In my mind's eye—golden rays project an aura from His Majesty the King

In my mind's eye—I can reach out and find His love in everything;

In my mind's eye— perfection from above truly makes my heart sing

In my mind's eye—I can remember…

Revised: (4-2011) - (11-2020)
--DWS

"COME AWAY"

Come away with me my Beloved...and I shall take you through still waters; that your joy may be full in me. You shall be washed with my grace that restores the soul;

Come away with me my Beloved...and I shall touch you with my finger of love; that your heart may sing aloud. You shall feel the essence of divinity and your soul shall be made free.

Come away with me my Beloved...and I shall take you beyond the horizon of the sea—where your spirit may soar above the clouds. You shall forever be in my presence as your soul longs for me.

Come away with me my Beloved...and I shall caress your heart with agape love—That your days on earth are prolonged. You shall feel my rainbow as it saturates you in the light.

Come away with me my Beloved...and I shall take you through the still waters—That your joy may be full always. You shall be washed with my grace that restores the soul and forever remains with me.

Come away with me my Beloved...Come away! #

CHAPTER 10
SPIRITUAL POEMS/PROSE SONG POEMS/LYRICS (PART 4)

"LIFE GOES ON"

Life goes on despite the isms and schisms

Life goes on despite our hurts and pains

Life goes on even if we agree to disagree

Life goes on just like the falling rain;

Life goes on despite sadness or melancholy

Life goes on when we are filled with joy

Life goes on within and without

Life goes on and will go on forevermore!

"PRAISE THE LORD"

Let the heavens and the earth proclaim the glory of the LORD and shout praises unto his name. Let the people praise and worship him because he is worthy of praise. Glory to the HIGHEST unto the LORD MOST HIGH!! He is the great KING and EVERLASTING FATHER and the PRINCE of PEACE. The LORD has gone up with a shout. Sing Hallelujah forevermore. Praise is comely and the Lord inhabits the praises of his people.

Lift your heads and clap your hands; sing praises unto the LORD. He is the "Alpha and Omega" our beginning and end. He is a bright and shining star. He is Jehovah Jireh our provider. He is the LORD Elyon, the MOST HIGH GOD. He is the LORD Jehovah El Shaddai who's more than enough the All-Sufficient One.

Glory Hallelujah is the highest praise in every tongue of every nation. Praise ye the LORD, make mention of his wondrous works to the children of men. Praise ye the LORD for great is the LORD and greatly to be praised.

Praise him with the cymbals, praise him with the high-sounding cymbals, and praise him with the timbrel and dance. Praise in the morning, praise Him in the noonday and praise him when the sun goes down. Let everything that has breath Praise the LORD, and bless his name forevermore.

Let the SWORD of the SPIRIT prevail against his enemies and let his righteous people rejoice! The LORD is strong and mighty; the LORD is mighty in battle. He is the KING, the KING of GLORY!! Praise him you people of the LORD! Yes, Praise him forevermore! #

"REVIVE"

Come forth and begin to shine;

Revive the consciousness of being

Bring light from out of the darkness

Walk in the pneuma and exhale excess

Express from your inner longing soul

Words from the divine that must be told

Revive—

Come forth and radiate His love

Revive true elements of peace

Bring hope from out of despair

Walk-in assurance without strife

Inhale joy and exhale sadness

Express a story to be unfolded

Words from the Divine that must be told

Revive—

"The distant past will make room for the future
In hopes that the present will endure until the end."
--Devon Wilford-Said
April' 2011

WHERE ANGELS FLY

The **LORD** strengthens my resolve and
brings my spirit into the light
Where angels fly far above the sky...
and my body has now taken flight;
The **LORD** strengthens my resolve and
brings my spirit into the light
As I lift my soul to worship him...throughout the day and night;
The **LORD** strengthens my resolve and
brings my spirit into the light
Where angels hearken to his commands...
and lift me right where I stand
The **LORD** strengthens my resolve and
brings my spirit into the light
Where angels fly far above the sky...
and my body has now taken flight
Amen. #

"EVENING IN FLIGHT"

One day I stood outside and watched the sun go down and wondered why it had left me; A still and eerie silence penetrated my soul as the orange florescent sky prepared itself for the night; I saw one lone star in the distance as it twinkled with rays of light that called out to me from above; Then suddenly my feet lifted slowly off the ground and my body began to move freely on one accord.

Did I think, wow— had I also defied the laws of gravity? As I became enchanted with my new found freedom when my spirit soared high in the night. Ever since I had returned my body continued to yearn for yet another beautiful *Evening in Flight*! #

*"Let the abundance of joy and love ignite
the flame of desire in your hearts,
And don't forget to share it with someone else in need of it."*

*"Time is measured from eternity for the
existence of man, but without
Positive change becomes stagnant and fruitless"*

--Devon Wilford-Said

"WORDS EMBRACE"

Lift me and caress me with the essence of your words

Take my hands—walk with me and show
me the way to true freedom

Talk to me with your words and teach
me from your spirit profound;

Strengthen me by letting me know with you that I can be strong

Look into my eyes—then grab hold of me and never let me go

Let me be in this moment always as your *words embrace* me so;

I love you…

"SHINE DOWN ON US"

Shine down on us spiritual rays that lighten our souls each day

Sift out from our emotions all pain and hurts from sadness;

Saturate our being with your pure joy and gladness

Shine down on us spiritual rays that will remove us from harm

Sift out from our hearts all bitterness, and hold us within your arms

Shine down on us with a pure heart before Heaven's throne;

Sift out from our minds negative thoughts
and help us to do no wrong

Saturate our being with the truth of your word even as a dove

Shine down on us spiritual rays of light and shower us with love;

CHAPTER 11
CREATIVE EXPRESSION (PART 1)

"I EXIST AND I AM WORD"

I exist because desires, emotions, and feelings must be expressed

I exist because thoughts from the mind are sometimes at unrest

I exist because uttered speech must be spoken by me

I exist because one must say what 's on the mind to be free

I exist in many languages, dialects and throughout the periods

I exist because I have the power to create from the heavenly divine

I exist because without me communication could not jive

I exist because *I Am Word* and I will be forever made alive—

Word Up! #

*"Be not afraid of sudden fear, neither of the desolation of
The wicked when it comes; for the Lord shall be your confidence,
And keep your foot from being taken."*
--Proverbs: 3: 25-26 KJV

"WHAT DO YOU FEAR?"

What do you fear?
A gruesome face with red eyes bulging through

What do you fear?
Or looking down from a real high place at the ground staring back up at you

What do you fear?
The shadow of death and, or being thrown down in the very pits of hell

What do you fear?
Or the wrinkles of time through your aging face and body cells

What do you fear?
A backstabbing, so-called friend who continues to slander you over and over again

What do you fear?
Or creepy things that always go bump, bump in the night

What do you fear?
A ghost or goblins that is sure to make anyone feel very uptight

What do you fear?
Someone looking over your shoulder when no one supposed to be there

What do you fear?

"From Within"

Or an evil witch's spell that is cast on you from out of nowhere

What do you fear?
The crash of your computer and the stock exchange with no money to be spent

What do you fear?
Or being evicted from your home because you can no longer pay the rent

What do you fear?
An avalanche, earthquake, tsunami, tornado, or hurricane

What do you fear?
Or the nasty words that were spoken from your mouth that cannot return again

What do you fear?
An instant betrayal from a loved one or even your best friend

What do you fear?
Or the doubt from someone's soul who is lost through rebellion and sin

What do you fear?
I do not have sudden fear because my warring angels are always near

*NOTE: Remember, to overcome fear we must have FAITH in God; and the faith of God. And to fear or reverence the Lord brings us wisdom to cast out any other fears outside of our faith.

> "The fear of the Lord is the beginning of wisdom and
> The knowledge of the holy is understanding."
>
> Proverbs: 9: 10 KJV

"DREAM MY DREAM"

I dream of a new reality a desire that many may think is unobtainable;
I dream of a day of peace and harmony and rest from hopelessness and despair

I dream of seeing the earth changed and brand new;
I dream of living with humanity without fear of being killed for naught

I dream of being able to fly and soar above the clouds without gravity's pullback down
I dream of sharing life with humanity, no matter what color or skin they happen to be in

I dream of immortality and the end of the 'fear of death' that we live forevermore
I dream of oneness with the Divine Creator and one day seeing Him face to face;

I dream of happy little children playing joyfully with their friends;
I dream of a new government established with peace, and love for everyone

I dream with the hope that one day I'll be able to see all my dreams become reality—#

"WHAT HAPPENS WHEN?"

What happens when?
The very thing that we thought would not happen, happens?

What happens when?
Wrong messages are sent to inquiring minds that need to know the truth

What happens when?
We're so sure that our point of view is correct, and then we find it's wrong

What happens when?
We open our mouths and no longer have a word to say

What happens when?
Your reality becomes unreal without any logical explanation

What happens when?
Your spirit has a personal relationship with the Holy Spirit

What happens when?
Love is unconditional and peace reigns forevermore

What happens when?
We allow unconditional love to happen?
Well one would think that all of them, "*what happens when* "would finally be put to rest #

"LIVE LIFE"

Life is to be lived as much as joy heals sorrow

Live life to the fullest and look forward to tomorrow;

Life is filled with so many endless

possibilities and choices for good

Live life and grow in God's good grace just as we all should…#

"SPRING FORTH"

Ah, the smell of a beautiful spring shower as the
morning dew trickles down blades of grass

The air is sweet with aromatic delights for a new day;

I can see new possibilities from budding trees as
flowering plants blooming within sight

Life is dancing all around me as the birds joyfully sing

Ah, the dayspring of warmth has embraced me as the amber rays

Of sun sneaked out from the clouds

The joy of pleasant things enlightens my path
for today as the dawning of hope

Springs forth I can see destiny and right choices within sight

Life is full and renewed into a glorious new day

"I AM GRATEFUL"

I am grateful for new beginnings;

And for every day that life comes forth

I am grateful for peace from within and joy from without

I am grateful for the love and giving love

I am grateful for abundance and sufficiency in all things

I am grateful for a free spirit to worship the

Almighty in 'Spirit and in Truth'

I am grateful for the life that

He has given both to me and for you;

I am and shall forever be so very grateful

"From Within"

"REJOICE O' EARTH"

Rejoice O' Earth so tried and true;
Let dews from heaven sparkle over you
Shine forth O' sun to present your light;
For winter's cold has now left from sight
Birds perched on limbs from the flowered nest
Sing melodies of a song to give their best
Rejoice O' Earth so tried and true;
Let the fragrances of spring comfort you
Shine forth O' sun too nurture this life
And erase all memoirs from misery and strife
Rejoice O' Earth from dawn to dust
In the Creator, we shall put our trust
Rejoice O' Earth, so tried and true
Let the fragrances of spring now comfort you
Shine forth O' sun and nurture cell life
Erase memories past from misery and strife
Sing praises with a song; you have passed the test
Now be awakened from winter's long weary rest
Rejoice O' Earth, Rejoice!

CHAPTER 12
CREATIVE EXPRESSION (PART 2)

"WHAT'S HAPPENING"

Spirit soars and leaves from time to time;
Mysteries of the unknown are misunderstood

Upheavals of despair mixed with spurts of hope
Weather patterns change now more frequently

Life is born into our world every second
Arms reach to embrace love from each other

Death closes shutters of windowless souls
Sorrow may come sometimes during the night

But joy seems to find its way in the morning
As crying souls starve for spiritual food

Technology and knowledge ahead of the race
Wisdom and understanding left far behind

Answers to question that won't be received
Love for a few and hate for so many

Egos and self-righteousness blinded by fear
I'm always right and you always wrong

But yet time continues to move on
Friends are hard to come by these days

Devon Wilford-Said

But diamonds in the ruff always shine through
When looking for light in the shadow of darkness

That's when the faith of God will bring us through
What's happening…?

"TODAY"

Today I stand in the reality of life and

Tomorrow who knows where I'll be;

Today I await a glimpse of hope

Amid troubled storms

Life ebbs on to its destined future

For tomorrow who knows what's in store

Today holds endless possibilities

Amid trials and tribulations

Today I await my dreams to come true

For tomorrows are never promised

And so, we always live for today;

Today…

"MY DAYS"

My days are like mountain spring water flowing downstream, and at times like rocks of bewilderment. As I reach out to embrace love from a body shivering from the cold, my heart sings out for relief.

How do you manage the things that you know not? Time seems to jaunt my very existence and I'm still searching hard for some answers.

My days are sometimes like endless nights of tossing and turning without sleep, and my body drenched in sweat. How do you find totality in a world filled with chaos? Do you span the globe for success through people that won't give you the time of day?

My mind spirit, soul, and body ache for something more pleasing and true.

Shall I search the heavens or reach for the stars? As my heart beats the drum for life, my soul cries out for the Creator.

My days have now been replaced from tears streaming down my face to new hope and confidence…#

"From Within"

"QUIET OF TIME"

Be still in the silence of now and entreat into the *Quiet of Time*;

Wait on his unchanging love and experience his excellent greatness

Allow the warmth to indwell your soul
with passion from spirit's flames

Listen to his Spoken Word and embrace the hope of your faith

Your joy shall be fulfilled and accepted
again in the *Quiet of Time…*

August-2005 Nov-2020
--DWS

Devon Wilford-Said

"MILES AHEAD"

Day by day we keep on seeking;
But we have miles ahead of our toll—
To reach the destinies of our lifetimes
And strive to perfect our highest goals;

Miles ahead in distance far
Miles ahead in time we are
Miles ahead…

Day by day we keep on growing
But we have miles ahead to go—
To become what we'd like to be
And yes, to know all that we should know

Miles ahead in distance far
Miles ahead in time we are
Miles ahead…

Day by day our lives are changing
But we have miles ahead of us still—
To live our lives unto the fullest
And to continue to do God's will

Miles ahead in distance far
Miles ahead in time we are
Miles ahead…

Revised: January 21, 1992-November 2020
The Best Poems of the '90s (Page 10)
The National Library of Poetry
ISBN 1-56167-035-9

"FEELINGS"

Laughter and joy pierce the soul and body when one is feeling in a good mood—

Sensations of warmth and love move through with elevated moments of bliss

A heart that rejoices and palpitates with satisfaction as being touched by fingers love

Ah—that's its total surrender from life's frustration and disappointments

Because now the body has awakened once more by its wonderful *feelings*—

"DO YOU KNOW?"

Do you know?

Do you know what you're feeling right now?

Do you understand the emotions from within?

Do you hear what's being said from above?

Do you want the best for your life, and those around you?

Do you cry for your voice to be heard when no one is listening?

Do you know what it takes for your success?

If so, then what do you know—do you know?

"From Within"

"ALIVE"

The breath of life as deeply inhaled
Ah—the collection of ethereal wind
Filia from lungs flaps joyously in and out

The banner of existence challenged for the dawn of a new day;
The sight from the portal of the soul with inner visions reflects lights of joy

Fingers touching the essences of feeling
Ears opened to hear the vibrating rhythm of sound

Feet planted solidly on earth's floor
Moving as directed by signals from the brain's waves

Nostrils breathe in its aromatic delights
From fragrant flowers along the path

Forward, ever projecting at life's steady pace
Skin cells are sensitized and refreshed;

Face radiant from the sun's warmth and glows
A body moves in sync with time that flows into eternity alive—

Revised:
May' 2011-2020 DWS

Devon Wilford-Said

"BREATHE INTO SPRING"

Breathe into Spring and sniff the fragrances of new life
Bursting into blossoms from flowers with prisms of vibrant colors

Breathe into Spring and let go of winter's toil of dark grey clouds
and cold blustery nights unfulfilled

Breathe into Spring as seasons change time after time;
In a world of doubts and fears from amidst life's struggles

Breathe into Spring against the backdrop of war and allow
peace to forever reign;

Breathe into Spring during the spiritual end-time events
Then despite it all allow joy to saturate your soul;

Breathe into Spring as children joyfully sing and play outside
under the warmth of the sun;

Breathe into Spring and allow love to overpower hate,
and unite hearts in peace

Breathe into Spring and your spirit shall soar once more
Rising higher into the presence of all that is and that shall be

Breathe into Spring and experience the newness of life and you
shall be rewarded by faith for an eternity

Breathe into Spring right now and continue to breathe—

"THE LIGHT"

The light that surrounds us shines forth from within us

The light that pierces darkness embraces us with its love

The light that radiates heat warms us from the cold

The light that heals us soothes our pain wrecked bodies;

The light that gives us life keeps us through all eternity

The light that illuminates the sky shines

forth throughout the heavens

The light that glows brilliantly shall be ignited to every soul;

The light that brings peace can also send war;

The light that shines forever shall always be with us

The light that's in everything shall forever reign as the light…#

CHAPTER 13
PROPHETIC UTTERANCE

"PROPHETIC UTTERANCES"

"CONFIRMATION OF THE LORD'S DIVINE PRESENCE"

Spoken through
The Late Min. /Prophet Ahmed B. Said
By the Unction of the Holy Spirit
Date: April 4, 2006

God is not hiding, and uses his prophets like a mouthpiece!
God is the essence of all things hoped for—
He is more than you could ever imagine
He is the inner peace within the peace. (Rehma)
God's promises; you can expect it because
it's going to birth forth like a baby
It will birth forth at the appointed time;
Revelation is to expose the *"will"* of God
We're his witnesses; his revealers!
That's our purpose to reveal the coming
of the Lord and what to expect
We're his extended speakers like a stereo player
Only as human enunciators, we're announcing
the coming of the LORD because,
He is coming to proclaim His victory! He is
coming—they'll have to know the truth
When God exposes Himself, it's awesome!

He does it with splendor and wonders…everything
He does stand out, and He does it
With such wonders that no force on earth can stop Him;
He can send tornadoes all over the place; destructive winds—
And yet He can time them into one place;
Don't tempt the Lord! Don't provoke Him to wrath
This is the force of the Lord, and He can do anything!
That only a few places get hit now and then—that's His miracles
His force, "the winds." He keeps them under His control
Don't provoke me to wrath, says the Lord
God is the master of them all, and He is awesome
That's how He displays Himself
The rainbow which displays His promise;
It's so beautiful with different magnificent colors
All of the colors are uniform and in an arc formation;
His firmament over the earth; He created the earth,
And He created the heavens too
No one controls anything except by His will;
Even the devil does not have control over God's will
Everything submits to Him; (light and darkness)
He overcomes the light—He overcomes the darkness
He is the "unexpected to be expected"
So, it is written, "The Revelation"
The Rehma, the Word, the Truth and Life
The more truth is revealed you will have more light
The truth is the light!
More truth, more light, and more clarity
Things will become clear, and it'll be so clear
That one day, you will see, God!
His plan just needs to come out;
If you absorb the truth—then you will comprehend the light
Walk upright into the light;
You will become brighter than the sun

"From Within"

Light represents cleansing and purity
To be cleansed you'd have to be purified
To get into heaven, you will have to be cleansed, and purified
Seek wisdom, seek the truth, and the truth shall set you free
That is how you will be free;
You will become more heavenly, purified, and cleansed
Thus, says the Lord, Amen, and Amen! ###

"AN EXHORTATION OF HOPE"

Inspired by the Holy Spirit
Spoken through Minister Devon Wilford-Said
Date: Friday, August 25th, 2006
Time: 11:19 AM

*"Ye are the children of the prophets, and of the
covenant which God made with our
fathers, saying, unto Abraham, And in thy seed shall
all the kindred's of the earth be blessed."*
Acts: 3: 25 KJV

*"For we cannot but speak the things which
we have seen and heard."*
Acts: 4: 20 KJV

PROPHECY

The refreshing of the Lord shall come upon you;

and you shall declare His Word with instruction unto the people.

Prophetic utterance shall fall from the lips of His prophets

and signs and wonders shall follow in these last days;

Remember what was written before and

the testimonies that followed.

And yea, yes the Lord God Himself shall

do a new thing in the earth.

This generation shall not pass away until it is revealed.

Says the Spirit of the Most High. Amen.

"LAST DAYS PROPHECY"

Inspired by the Holy Spirit
Spoken through Minister Devon Wilford-Said
Date: Tuesday, October 10th, 2006
Time: 9: 45 AM

*"And I will pour upon the house of David
and the inhabitants of Jerusalem
the spirit of grace and of supplications;
and they shall look upon me
whom they have pierced, and they shall mourn for His only son,
and shall be in bitterness for him, as one that
is in bitterness for his firstborn"*
Zechariah: 12: 10 KJV

*"And it shall come to pass afterward,
that I will pour out of my spirit
upon all flesh; and your sons and your daughters shall prophesy,
your old men shall dream dreams; your
young men shall see visions:
And also upon the servants and upon the handmaids
in those days will I pour my Spirit? And I
will show wonders in the heavens
and in the earth, blood, and fire, and pillars of smoke."*
Joel: 2: 28-30 KJV

PROPHETIC UTTERANCE

Beloved, rejoice and praise the Lord your God; Praise him and give Him the glory that is due to His Name. For the Lord has heard the cries of His people. He shall lift you out of the dunghills of languishing. He will heal you of your diseases, and set you on high. The Lord has given you His Spirit to perform exploits and deliverance for those in need. He has sent you the comforter to comfort your broken-hearted, and to lift you out of your despair.

The Lord is your strong tower of safety and you can run to Him and be safe. He will smite the hands of the enemy that goes up against His anointed, His Chosen. Rejoice in the Lord your God, for He, shall do mightily in the earth and on behalf of His people. Hold fast your confidence in Him for you shall be rewarded double for your faithfulness. In the night season, He shall seal His instructions as you slumber and sleep.

Weeping may endure for a night, but joy shall come forth in the morning. You are the Lord's beloved and His desire are towards you. At the gates are all manner of pleasant fruit for His people, his chosen and you shall be a crown of glory in the hand of the Lord. Yes, you shall be a royal diadem in the hand of your God.

Be still and know your God for it is He that gives you the abundance of blessing; it is He who has blessed the works of your hand and delivered you from destruction?

Rejoice O' daughters and sons of the Most High because you shall triumph and reign in the kingdom forever. The LORD strong and mighty, the Lord mighty in battle shall conquer His enemies and smite them with the word of His mouth. And His people shall live victoriously with Him in the New Jerusalem. Hold fast to these words and remain faithful even until the end, says the Lord God of Hosts. Amen and amen. #

"HIDDEN BUT NOT SECRET"

"Thus, says the LORD, the Holy One of Israel, and his Maker, ask me of things to come concerning my sons, and concerning the works of my hands command you me. I have made the earth, and created man upon it; I, even my hands have stretched out the heavens, and their entire host have I commanded." Isaiah: 45: 11-12 KJV

Spoken Through
Minister Devon Wilford-Said
By the
Unction of the Holy Spirit

PROPHECY

Behold, says the LORD, some things can be known and some things are not yet ready to be revealed. At the appointed time, all shall be known that have been hidden from times past. "For the secret things belongs to me," says the LORD; and that thing that shall be revealed belongs to you and your children.

Wait on the LORD, your GOD, and take joy in Him; for the LORD knows every secret thing, and there's nothing hidden that shall not come to light. Call unto me and I shall answer you. I shall teach you the things promised from my WORD.

You shall know that that I am the LORD, your GOD, and your strength shall be made perfect in your weakness. For wisdom shall be the stability of your times; now is the time for salvation; now is your faith. Take hold of it, walk in it, and do my will on the earth. You shall prosper and every need shall be supplied according to my riches and glory.

Behold, the earth is mine, says the LORD; and everything made that was made. You are mine the work of my hands for which I am well pleased. I shall refine you and try you through the furnace of afflictions, but you shall come forth as pure gold.

You are my jewels says, the LORD. So, let your light shine to reveal my glory that's upon you. Yes, a rise and shine always, and my glory shall radiate upon your stature; and I will be with you always, even until the end.

Behold, I show you a mystery—that which cannot be explained. I will confound every man that thinks that he knows me by intellectual thinking, says the LORD. Yes, for man's wisdom is foolishness to me.

But I will bring you in a way that you know not; that man shall see and know that I am the LORD and that I am with you! My favor shall rest upon you, and everyone that comes in contact with you shall see my glory upon you. Walk faithfully and stay obedient to my Word. Do the work of an evangelist, and make full proof of your ministry that I have ordained and given to you. I love you, O' Daughters and Sons of Zion take joy! And peace is with you, says the Spirit of the LORD of Host! Amen and Amen.

"KEEP THE FAITH"

"Now faith is the substance of things hoped for, the evidence of things not seen."
Hebrews: 11:1 KJV

"Now FAITH is the assurance (the confirmation, the title deed) of things [we] hope for, being the proof of things [we] do not see and the conviction of their reality [faith perceiving as real fact what is not revealed to the senses]."
Hebrews: 11:1 AMP

"Now faith is the substantiation of things hope for, the conviction of things not seen."
Hebrews: 11:1 [The New Testament Recovery Version]

A PROPHETIC EXHORTATION TO MY BELOVED

"My Beloved you must forge ahead with full assurance and hope, but most of all with faith. I say unto you, "The just shall live by his faith, and walk upright before the LORD."

Believe in the LORD your God and be established; believe his prophets and so shall you prosper. It takes faith to believe and to trust in the LORD; I say unto you believe on the Lord Jesus Christ, and if you haven't already given your life to HIM, call him, confess and repent of Your sins and be saved. The LORD loves you and will abundantly pardon; he will renew your mind and set you free! If you have faith as a mustard seed and no doubt you can say to this mountain be you removed and be cast into the sea.

Dare to have faith to love the LORD your GOD with all your heart, strength, and might. Dare to have faith to love your neighbor as yourself.

Dare to have faith to remove mountains and overcome every stumbling block or obstacle. Dare to have faith to fulfill your destiny and purpose in GOD.

Dare to have faith to live a righteous life in this world, and in the one to come! Dare to have faith to lay hands on the sick that they may recover.

Dare to have the faith to cast out demons and set the captives free. Dare to have faith to *"do"* the impossible with GOD! Dare to have the faith to encourage others and to endure, even until the end. Dare to have faith to be strong in the LORD's might and to keep the faith!"

In the mighty name of Jesus Christ, have faith and *Keep the Faith* in GOD!"

Amen and Amen.

CHAPTER 14

THOUGHTS PRAYERS/ MORE POETRY (PART 1)

"KNOCK AND THE DOOR SHALL BE OPENED"

"Ask, and it will be given to you; seek and you will find; *"knock and the door will be opened to you."* For everyone who asks receives, he who seeks finds; *and to him who knocks, the door will be opened."* Matthews: 7:7-8 NIV

"Here I am! *I stand at the door and knock.* If anyone hears my voice and opens the door, I will come in and eat with him, and he with me." Rev: 3:20 NIV

When I first began to seriously get into the Word of God, I found that one of my favorite scriptures was at that time found in the Book of Matthew, Chapter 7; and verses 7-8.

Yes, it was all about the "asking, seeking, and knocking" which led me to believe that God was truly listening to my many prayer petitions to him as a child. Back then my mom had told me and my sisters to read the 23rd Psalm and to recite our nightly prayers for protection. You know that familiar prayer that most children had to say before going to sleep each night.

"Now I lay me down to sleep, I pray the LORD, my soul to keep;

And if I should die before I awake; I pray the LORD, my soul to take." Amen.

My grandmother once said that I was a special child; and that I was called out for the LORD's purpose. She constantly told me not to fear, but to always trust in the LORD. When I first opened the door of my heart to allow the LORD to come in I was around twelve years of age.

It was a wonderful feeling of love and acceptance and making that choice was the best thing I could ever do. When I was baptized and filled with the Holy Spirit some years later, I was overjoyed and very thankful that I had done the right thing and made the right choice.

I hope that anyone who may be reading this message, and who has not yet answered the LORD's call that they'd reconsider; and open the door of their hearts and allow Him to come in.

"I will open my mouth in a parable: I will utter dark sayings of old; which we have heard and known, and our Fathers have told us. We will not hide them from their children, showing to the generations to come to the praises of the LORD, and his strength, and the wonderful works that he has done."
--Psalm: 78:2-4 KJV

"With my soul have I desired thee in the night; yea, with my spirit within me will I seek thee early: for when your judgments are in the earth, the inhabitants of the world will learn righteousness."
--Isaiah: 26:9 KJV

"You will keep him in perfect peace whose mind is stayed on thee because he trusts in thee. Trust in the LORD forever, for the LORD JE-HO-VAH is everlasting strength."
--Isaiah: 26: 3-4 KJV

"THE LORD'S PEACE"

PRAYER

Father, we seek you in the name of Jesus for our sustenance and peace. We love you LORD, and desire to walk closer with you. Grant your servants the grace that's needed to perform your will in the earth.

We thank you, LORD because we're aware of your presence and your guidance with each breath that we take. We glorify you LORD because you are to be glorified for your goodness sake.

In the name of Jesus, the name that is above every name, we thank and praise you for your promises towards your servants that perform your will in the earth. Be glorified O' Righteous Father and Judge. Be glorified because you are worthy from the foundation of the universe and throughout all eternity.

As we continue to keep our minds stayed on you…be glorified always, Father! We love and salute your name to the highest, Glory Hallelujah to you both now and forevermore in Jesus name, we pray. Amen and Amen.

> *"I will therefore that men pray everywhere,*
> *lifting up holy hands, without wrath and doubting."*
> 2 Timothy: 2: 8 KJV

"HIS LOVE FOR US"

There is a need in these last days for all people to come to the knowledge of the truth concerning a loving Heavenly Father who gave of Himself to be touched by the feelings of everyone's infirmities. A Savior if you please that wants the best for every human being that dwells on the face of this earth. A loving Savior that has shed His precious blood through much pain and suffering; and even death on the cross taking on the sins of the world. And yet, not for Himself but for us, He laid down His life so freely. It is so good to know that He died that we might have life and that more abundantly to justify our right relationship again with the Heavenly Father, Hallelujah! Yes, Jesus (Yeshua) the Christ and the anointed of God, the Messiah and Savior sacrificed His life for us. The Father loved us so much that He had to redeem us from an ill fate of sin and eternal death from being separated from Him.

Love is so powerful and we need His unconditional love to survive in this life and through death for which we all headed one day. Even though there will be only a few that will acknowledge and accept His wonderful gift of love. By believing the word of faith that is preached; that if we confess with the mouth the Lord Jesus, and believe in their hearts that God raised him from the dead, to be saved. For whosoever calls on the name of the Lord shall be saved. Yes, the Heavenly Father loved us so much that He gave His only begotten Son that whosoever should believe in Him they would inherit eternal life. Now that's love at its best, an unconditional love I would say—Thank you, Lord! #

"TREES OF RIGHTEOUSNESS"

Rejoice O' Sons and Daughters of the Most High for you belong to the LORD! And He has planted you firmly within his kingdom. He has sure up your foundation so that wisdom and knowledge can be the stability of your times.

The winds may blow and sway you from side to side. But if you're rooted and grounded in His love and faith---you shall not be moved! For, He has established you and His right-hand does mightily on your behalf.

PRAYER

Heavenly Father in the Name of Jesus,

As a tree that is planted and rooted by the rivers of water begins to grow up to its full stature and grace with extended branches like arms reaching out to embrace, and limbs that houses many fowls of the air. And whose shade covers man from the heat of the sun on a hot summer day and that bears him fruit for to eat.

You have looked upon us as you're *"Trees of Righteousness* or one who has right-standing with you to be able to inherit the promises of your faithful servant Abraham, the Father of all nations.

A tree signifies strength, endurance, and stability because it has to be rooted and grounded into the earth to endure high winds and storms from season to season. We as believers too must be rooted and grounded but, in your Word, to overcome the storms, trials and tribulations, and many afflictions of this life. Thank you, Lord, for your wonderful gift of life, and as we continue to grow in grace through faith strengthen us to endure unto the end.

In Jesus, Name is my prayer. Amen. #

CHAPTER 15
THOUGHTS PRAYERS/ MORE POETRY (PART 2)

"PRAY WITHOUT CEASING"

*"Rejoice forevermore, pray without ceasing.
In everything give thanks for this is the will of God in
Christ Jesus, concerning you."*
I Thessalonians: 5: 16-18 KJV

Father, in the Name of Jesus,

You said, in your Word that *"Men ought to always pray, and not to faint"* therefore I, (We), petition you with this heartfelt prayer according to your will in faith believing that you always honor the prayers of the righteous.

I, (We) thank you Lord for lifting up our spirits and easing the pain of grief and sorrow; and the many persecutions afflicted upon your people for doing that which is right.

I, (We), thank you Lord for the forgiveness of sin and your mercy and grace. I, (We), trust that all things are in your hands and that you shall reward the adversaries against your people their just rewards. Our earth is plagued with hatred and violence and the oppression of the poor and needy.

Many rich in the land have turned their backs on the people of low estate. You said, that *"the earth is the Lord's and the fullness thereof, the world and they who dwell therein."* But, yet so many of your people still suffer lack because of the selfishness of the wicked.

Despite what I, (We), suffer we shall yet praise your Name because you rain down on the just and the unjust. And you said, *"But my God shall supply all your need according to His riches in glory by Christ Jesus our Lord."* I, (We) lift you now with the highest praise which is, Glory Hallelujah! I, (We), bless your name forevermore.

In, Jesus name Amen and amen. #

"WHO AM I?"

Who Am I? I AM the presence of power from on high
Who Am I? I AM the Master and Creator from heaven's sky

Who AM I? I made you in my image to be my delight
Who AM I? I brought you from darkness into my marvelous light

Who Am I? I AM He that stands at your heart's door and knock
Who Am I? I AM holy with perfection and let no man dare mock

Who Am I? I AM the Father that gave my Son to show you, my love
Who AM I? Who suffered bled and died for sin then ascended above

Who Am I? If you turn from your sins and be baptized in My Name
Who Am I? You'll be given a new life, and will never be the same

Who Am I? Obedience to My Word and faith shall set you free
Who Am I? Faith is all it takes if you'd be truly willing to please me

Who Am I? I AM your Salvation and more closely than a friend
Who Am I? And if you refuse to obey you will die in your sins

Who Am I? If you'd accept My Holy Spirit you shall have power too
Who Am I? Perform miracles, wonders, and even greater things shall you do?

Who Am I? I AM that I AM…

PRAYER

Father, in the Name of Jesus,

I thank you that you're I AM that I AM and that you are all that we need you to be!

I thank you for our Lord and Savior Jesus Christ who died on our behalf that we can now stand

before your Holy presence and worship, you in love. You are everything to me and I praise

you for being just Who You are…The Great I AM that I AM in Jesus name, Amen.

"FROM WITHIN"

During mankind's existence here on earth, we have been in constant battles and inner struggles *"from within"* our minds. And to be able to have control of our bodies, soul, and spirit; at times seems incomprehensible. So much so that the mind begins to think of certain ways to please itself based on its egotistical means of self-expression. This process usually causes many of us to get out of sync with our true identity as human beings.

God has fashioned us to become unique individuals with purpose free will and with an inability to fulfill our destiny by advancing us forward to allow growth in knowledge and wisdom! We were given the charge to have dominion over the earth cultivate it, and subdue it! He gave man skills and the will to accomplish anything that he sets his mind to do—after all was not man created in God's image? (Genesis: 1: 27 KJV)

Our brain was designed to control all functions of the body's operations. The mind which is housed within is the communication and activity center responsible for directing all conscious and subconscious thought. But just how does one come to terms with one's own mind? The most complicated and unusual part of his or her makeup—Well, Webster's Collegiate dictionary describes the part of the mind which is called, consciousness, as (the quality or state of being aware of something within one's self) or the self-conscious which depicts having mental faculties un-dulled by sleep, faintness, or stupor.

Thus, the conscious state in short is being awake and capable of or marked by thought. Then there's the subconscious reality, which is described as (existing in the mind, but not immediately available to consciousness) whereby the mental activities is just below the threshold of consciousness, if I may?

Yes, and of course we have the mind itself which is described as (the element or complex of elements in an individual that feels, perceives, thinks, wills, and reason).

The mind deals with different behaviors and mental processes. I'm sure that most Psychologists would agree based on their analytical research to search out the intricate details.

Sometimes I question why and how a man's brain can hold so much internal and, external information in it—do his thoughts and behaviors fluctuate by choice, or is it done by force through thought projections conceived from outside influences?

There's so much to learn about this most fascinating subject however, my focus, for now, deals strictly with the intuitive or creative abilities of one's mind. The aspect of one's character that controls his abilities to ascertain just who he or she is, and that which comes *from within*. And is the part that cannot be seen however that is touched by the Spirit of the Creator. This is the part that cries out daily to be connected to His first love!

For within man is a spirit that cries out to identify with our Heavenly Father. "But there is a spirit in man and the inspiration of the Almighty gives them understanding."
(Job: 32: 8 KJV)

In closing, I've found that the mind must be able to express and process all the creative and inspirational knowledge that it has received for the whole man to be complete. Therefore, man should be willing to deal with all the negatives elements that center upon his ego and sometimes not so positive way of thinking. To embrace the wonderful creative complexities of his person and remain open-minded to the things of the Lord His God!

Prayer:

"Father in the name of Jesus give us a mind to want to know you from within, and without is my prayer that you may be glorified always." Amen and amen.

"THINK ABOUT IT"

The world's a changing every minute of the hour and second of the day—Into a fallen society of power-hungry souls that is not in control; To usurp their authority over others less fortunate than they—Where the love of money roots out its evil to destroy everyone and everything in its way; Powerful corporate men hoarding and manipulating funds over and over again; But to the poor and oppressed and those in bad health—They dare not share even a small portion of their wealth; Let the poor remain poor so what do they care? Hey…he got his and they got theirs, and no one is really going anywhere!

Think about it…

The world's changing every minute of the hour and second of the day—Widespread pollution of the environment that destroys everything good that God has made; Factory smoke, exhaust from cars, buses, and trucks; And nuclear threats from third world countries have run amuck; Earthquakes in many places shaking up the earth's foundation's core; A greenhouse effect with no ozone layer to protect from the sun; Wars and rumors of wars that cannot be won—El Nin'no tidal waves causing overflowing oceans, rivers, and lakes; Hurricanes and tornados hurl debris from one town to the next and from state to state;

Think about it…

The world's changing every minute of the hour and second of the day—Men and women joy in pornography and burning in their lust; Raping, killing, and stealing for a green paper that reads, "In God We Trust;" Babies having babies, invitro-sterilizations, abortions, and Pro-Choice; Scientists cloning humans…Hey, what has happened to God's voice?

Other strange phenomena, the psychic connection they ought to know; People running to and fro to obtain knowledge for a better way to go—It's the computer age cyberspace and high-tech to keep us ahead; While oppression, sickness, and diseases such as AIDS that's dropping them dead; Religious fanatics are on the rise with heavy burdens that cannot set free—In a lost world from purity and love; And we know that is not at all the way Our Creator ever intended it to be!

Think about it...

Prayer:

Father in the name of Jesus, as the world continues to change please give us the strength to endure the hardness of our lives. We are subject to be here until the consummation of all things and we need your guidance and courage to stand during these perilous times. Give us your grace and mercy to hold on. In Jesus' name, Amen and amen.

"AUTHOR'S CLOSING REMARKS"

"This spirit of mine— is flying high;
This spirit of mine— goes beyond the sky
This spirit of mine— knows what's in store
This spirit of mine—free forevermore"

By: **Devon Wilford-Said**
--November'1978

"Whosoever shall confess that Jesus is the Son of God, God dwells in him, and he in God; And we have known and believed the love that God has to us. God is love, and he that dwells in love dwells in God and God in him." I John: 4: 15-16 KJV

"I pray that this book has been an encouragement to you the reader and that you have been blessed by its contents because it has been an honor and pleasure to give back what the Lord has parted in me to glorify Him.

We all need to be uplifted from time to time and having a good book to read, or to be listened to as well thanks to the new audible books now available in our book stores; can truly enhance the quiet moments of relaxation and meditation.

Just remember that you are important to the Lord; and that He wants you to enjoy the intimacy of His presence as one that opens his mind and heart to receive the unconditional love of his or her Father that comes, *"From Within."*

Peace and Blessings Always,

Min. Devon Wilford-Said

The Author

www.ingramcontent.com/pod-product-compliance
Lightning Source LLC
Chambersburg PA
CBHW072015110526
44592CB00012B/1319